D0745595

A Life in Writing

A Life in Writing

The Story of an American Journalist

CHARLES CHAMPLIN

Syracuse University Press

Copyright © 2006 by Syracuse University Press
Syracuse, New York 13244–5160
All Rights Reserved

First Edition 2006
06   07   08   09   10   11   6   5   4   3   2   1

Library of Congress Cataloging-in-Publication Data
Champlin, Charles, 1926–
A life in writing : the story of an American journalist / Charles
Champlin.—1st ed.
p. cm.
ISBN 0–8156–0847–0 (cloth : alk. paper)
1. Champlin, Charles, 1926– 2. Journalists—United States—
Biography. I. Title.
PN4874.C43A3   2006
070.92—dc22   2006000029

Manufactured in the United States of America

 This book is for my brother, Joe, who figures so largely in it.

Charles Champlin was a working journalist from the time he graduated from Harvard College in 1948 until his retirement in 1991. Born in Hammondsport, New York, in 1926, Champlin served two years in the infantry in World War II before taking up his career as a journalist. From 1948 to 1965, he was a reporter, correspondent, and writer for *Life* and *Time* magazines in New York, Chicago, Denver, Los Angeles, and London. He has been the arts editor and a columnist for the *Los Angeles Times* since 1965 and was also the newspaper's principal film critic between 1967 and 1980. He met his wife in the Hammondsport Public Library and married her in St. Gabriel's Church. They have six children, thirteen grandchildren, and four great-grandchildren.

Contents

Illustrations

Preface

I t seemed presumptuous of me in 1989 to publish a memoir covering only the first sixteen years of my life and assume that anyone
would want to read it. Yet, for me, those years had a beginning, a
middle, and an abrupt ending when my mother remarried and we
moved away from the village where the family had lived for a century. And as it turned out, that memoir, *Back There Where the Past Was,*
along with the newspaper columns that gave rise to it, had reso-
nances for many people who had never heard of me or of Hammondsport, Steuben County, New York.

The idea of the settled small town where almost everyone knew
almost everyone else had a strong nostalgic appeal at a time when, as
I said in the book, we are all from someplace else and we cherish a
past we have left behind.

I often heard from readers of my earlier book that they found
strong echoes of their own towns and their own histories in places as
remote from Hammondsport as a Brooklyn neighborhood or a hamlet in the wheat fields of North Dakota. I had celebrated the way of
life in a small village in the 1930s and up to our participation in
World War II. Villages then were nearly all self-contained as they
never would be again. The settled continuity of village life, as in
Hammondsport, was to be disrupted and changed forever—by the
foretastes of war, by the war itself, and by the great shifts of popula-

tion resulting from the war and from increasing prosperity and job relocations in the postwar world. An era of village life had ended.

After the murderous attacks of 9/11, I called a historian friend of mine in New York City. He said that he and his family were safe and unharmed. But, he added, "The world I grew up in and was very fond of has disappeared forever." It was exactly so; we had all been severed from our past. We had lost an enveloping confidence and feeling of security that had survived all the dark times the country had known.

At first, I was not sure that this account of a young man growing up in wartime and seeking a career in the early postwar years would have the same interest for readers that the first volume proved to have. As I wrote, however, I began to sense that my own experiences of military service and combat, of college and first love, and simply being part of a fast-changing society might well reflect hopes and fears and aspirations that were by no means exclusive to me. If this memoir fits in a genre known as the "coming of age" book, it might also be seen as a report on the coming of age of a whole society adjusting to a lost innocence, but with defiant and undiminished hope.

My own rites of passage have been driven by a passion to write that began when I was barely Boy Scout age and that has never diminished.

Charles Champlin

Acknowledgments

M idway through the first draft of the book I was afflicted by age-related macular degeneration (AMD) which literally overnight left me legally blind, unable to drive a car, and unable to read, and it made the process of revising and polishing the text difficult indeed.

My daughter Susan Champlin, formerly managing editor of *Modern Maturity* and *Bon Appetit,* came to my rescue. She read the manuscript twice, mading innumerable suggestions that amounted to a fine polish on the text. I am forever indebted to her for her enthusiastic but careful eye.

Any memoir borrows the eyes and the memories of many friends and relatives. I owe particular thanks to my brother, Monsignor Joseph Masson Champlin of Syracuse; our sister, Nancy Haynes Kreis of New York; and my cousin Deborah Fisher of Canandaigua, New York, for some wonderful photographs and historical information about my stepfather's family. I owe special thanks to former sergeant John Babcock of Ithaca, New York, for his good counsel and encouragement in combat in the winter of 1945 and years later for a useful letter of reminiscence about a tense time for both of us above the Roer River.

I am most grateful to Carol Stewart, my secretary, to whom I dictated much of the later stages of the book and who was wonderfully patient with my frequent revisions. She also laughed in appropriate places, to my great relief.

Above all, I give profound thanks to my wife, Peggy, who was an unusually discerning critic and who steered the manuscript through the mysteries of the computer.

A Life in Writing

Leaving

When last seen, I was driving my grandmother's 1937 Buick Century northeast from Hammondsport, New York, where I'd lived all my life, to an even smaller town, named Cleveland, that I'd never seen, a hamlet on the north shore of Oneida Lake. It was July 1942, and I was to begin a new life with a stepfather I scarcely knew. I was in a real whipsaw of emotions, separating from a place I loved and feeling a mixture of apprehension, only faintly tinged with excitement, about a new place, a new family unit, a future likely to be quite different from any I'd envisioned in Hammondsport.

It was in Hammondsport that I, at age ten or so, had determined that writing would be central to my destiny. I'd figured out that I would never make it as a professional shortstop, much less a professional cornet player, so that by process of elimination, I knew that my future had to be as a writer, however I arrived at that exalted status. Always a hungry reader, I discovered early the joys of language, and spent my teenage years running barefoot through them.

Leaving Hammondsport and driving toward a new life in a new house and a new school in a new town, I was starting all over again, minus the security of my family past and all the comforts of a long family history in Hammondsport. I was probably lonelier than I'd ever felt in my life, and lonelier than I would ever feel again. It seemed to me that I was en route from one destiny to another. It may be that this was the first time I was even dimly aware that my ability to write was a skill and a comfort I could fall back on to see me through whatever the years ahead held for me. In a sense, it was my pencil (or my typewriter) that stood between me and the darkness.

Next to me in the car was my grandmother, Nancy Wheeler Masson, a petite and sprightly widow, then, I suppose, in her early sixties. In the family she was always called "Nano." Her mother had been abandoned by her father when Nano was two; her father was never to be seen again, and her mother had died when Nano was only ten. She was adopted by Judge Monroe Wheeler of Hammondsport, whose wife was Nano's aunt, her mother's sister. Nano and her husband, Leon Joseph Masson, had had one child, my mother, Katherine Marietta Masson.

My mother had been raising my younger brother, Joe, and myself as a single parent since my father had left when I was six and Joe was two. They were divorced when I was about eight, and my father died on Christmas morning when I was twelve. Mother was a beautiful woman all her life. She had dark hair and brown eyes, and the portraits of her as a young woman suggest an almost classic elegance. She'd graduated as valedictorian of her small high school class at Hammondsport and gone on to Vassar, finishing in the class of 1922. She and my father married in 1925—one of those marriages seemingly made in heaven, but concluded elsewhere. During the early thirties, when the family winery, Pleasant Valley, was moribund thanks to Prohibition, she and we somehow scraped along. She worked briefly at the winery when it restarted after Repeal, and for several years was a teller at the Bank of Hammondsport. Then—and I suppose it was toward end of 1941—Charles Harold Haynes of Cleveland, New York, asked her to marry him. Mother sought permission from Joe and me. If for any reason we had rejected the idea, I'm sure she would have gone along with our feelings. Perhaps more than Joe, who was not yet twelve, I was aware of the loneliness of her life and the curious small-town mixture of sympathy and separateness with which she lived. We wished her all the happiness she deserved. She and Charles Haynes were married in Hammondsport on June 1, 1942. I gave Mother away.

After a brief honeymoon, Mother and her new husband had stopped in Hammondsport to pick up my brother, Joe, and take him to Cleveland. I'd stayed on with Nano recuperating from my appendectomy. On a bright, lovely early July morning, Nano backed the car, which we'd loaded the night before, out of the driveway and we headed up Vine Street. We passed the big yellow three-story house my great-grandfather Masson had built in the last century and swung onto Lake Street. I knew every house we passed, of course: the Grimaldis', Sherm Wright's, the Converys', Fred and Harriett Taylor's on the left, and then, with a particular tug at my heart, 51 Lake Street, the small two-story white house with the Greek Revival roofline where I'd lived all of my life until now. The Civil War monument with the statue of a Union soldier on top then still stood in the middle of the intersection of Lake and Main Streets, and my grandmother made a wide turn around it and went over Main Street to Sheather (as it was then spelled). We passed all the familiar buildings: Hemmer's hardware, the town library, Ethel Wooding's dry goods shop, the Market Basket, the A&P, the post office, Smellie's drugstore, and the Park Inn. We bent around the village square with the bandstand where I used to tootle on Saturday nights in summer, and out past Mike Canteloupe's garage—where Mike made sure my grandmother had enough gas to get to Cleveland and back—then onto Route 54.

Just out of town, Nano pulled the Buick to the side of the road. The highway was slightly elevated there and I could look down at Put's Dock at the end of Keuka Lake, where we swam in the summertime. Alongside the dock were the high old boathouses from which the most daring teenagers used to dive.

Nano said, "I'd like you to drive." I'd never driven a car more than a few yards back and forth in her driveway. She either didn't know that or chose to ignore it on the grounds that driving the car would overwhelm whatever else I was feeling. If so, she was right. Exciting as it was, the driving knotted my stomach like a gourd and pushed all other concerns out of my head. The Buick had a stick shift, with which I'd had no actual road experience at all. I knew where the gears were because, when I was younger, a morose fellow named Barton used to let me shift the gears on his pickup while he delivered groceries for Herman Harder's market. But Barton had always worked the clutch, and it took me most of the trip to Cleveland to get the hang of it. My grandmother looked pained but kept bravely silent each time the gears made that dreadful grinding sound.

I headed north along Route 54, which is close to the lake most of the way to Branchport. We passed the Masson cottage, where Joe and I spent a couple of weeks each summer, in company with our great-uncle Victor and our three maiden great-aunts, Tillie, Julie, and Josie, who swam each afternoon in their knee-length bathing costumes, which even then spoke of an earlier time. A few miles beyond the cottage was Lakeside, the small amusement park where the school picnics were held each year. There was a roller rink and a slide so high you could ride a board down it into the lake at great speed. You could; I never dared. There was also a chained bear who slept in a concrete drainage pipe and who, I think, drank itself to death on bottles of pop provided by visitors.

I negotiated my first two stop lights in Penn Yan with a minimum of grinding and we ran east through some lovely farm country. We had never had a car of our own—Mother's own, that is—and I had rarely traveled those lovely hills between the Finger Lakes, with their postcard vistas of barns, silos, tidy farmhouses, and wide fields of corn, now more than knee-high as we drove by. In the distance, I caught glimpses of the sparkling water of the next of the Finger Lakes, Seneca, where we turned onto Route 14 and again headed north to Geneva, with its rows of glorious town houses dating back almost to the Revolutionary War. One of the stop lights in Geneva was on a grade, where I managed to grind, stall, and grind again until I finally made it through the green light and up the slope. My grandmother looked particularly anxious during this episode, but bless her heart, she didn't say a word.

We were now, I suppose, an hour into the trip and I'd undergone a kind of emotional metamorphosis. The romantic wrench I'd felt as I had my last look at Hammondsport was beginning to be replaced by a rising interest in what I was seeing now. In my most dramatic moments, my imaginings were that I'd left warmth, security, and happiness behind me, and possibly my future hopes as well, and would forever after be a loner in alien surroundings. This, naturally, proved to be gross and self-pitying nonsense. It did not take into account the universal resilience and optimism of the young. It did, however, nourish the would-be writer's sense of himself as an outsider, someone set apart—the better vantage point from which to view the world and comment upon it.

We drove past the frightening reaches of Montezuma Swamp, a magnificent sanctuary for migratory birds, but in its watery desolation, without structures or people, it was more than a little scary. The next hurdle was Syracuse, where I had not only to struggle with the Buick but also to pick my way around the fringes of the city and onto Route 15. I headed north, catching my first glimpse of Oneida Lake and crossing over the Barge Canal at Brewerton. At Central Square, I turned east onto Route 49 and drove through a succession of pretty, diminutive villages—West Monroe, Constantia, and Bernhards Bay. Here the road runs right along the lake. On the hill above the road a pleasant house commanded a wonderful view of the picturesque shoreline, and my stepfather later told me that the novelist Hervey Allen had leased the house when he was writing his bestseller in the thirties, *Anthony Adverse*.

My senses were alert, like an explorer's in a distant land. Nothing was radically different, of course; I was covering perhaps 130 miles within the same state. Barns were red, houses were white, the trees were maples and, still in those days, elms. The differences I perceived were slight, almost nuances. The soil in plowed fields looked redder and sandier. There were expanses of scrubby second-growth woods, pines contending with alders. The countryside to the north seemed emptier and somehow more rural. To the south, you couldn't see across the wide expanse of the lake, which gave it, as I thought, a kind of impersonal austerity, quite unlike Keuka Lake, which is hardly a mile wide at its broadest.

That pleasant summer morning could have been any pleasant summer morning, but quite beyond my own uncertainties and anxieties, this was wartime, seven or eight months after the Japanese had attacked Pearl Harbor, and a much larger uncertainty hung above us all. Already some of my slightly older friends in Hammondsport had gone into service. On a few frosty mornings, I'd gone up to Bath and played in what we called the "Draft Band," escorting the draftees from the village square to the railroad depot. Their mothers and other womenfolk came down to see them off, with the tears mostly held back until the train had pulled out. The train took them to the terminus at Hoboken, where they changed for Fort Dix.

I drove slowly to the village of Cleveland and its handful of stores and houses. Two miles east of the village, we spotted my stepfather's white house, identified by two towering elm trees in the front yard. It was a small farmhouse, probably the better part of a century old, with a wide porch across the front and fields on either side. Behind the house was a small garage and, beyond it, an enormous barn; up a gentle slope beyond the barn began a wood lot that ran north as far as the eye could see. Mother and Joe came out of the house to greet us and help us unload.

Pop

Years later, I realized far more sharply than I did at the time what an act of courage it was for my stepfather to marry for the first time that summer of all summers. Charles Harold Haynes was a thirty-eight-year-old bachelor, my mother, forty-two. He was acquiring not only a wife but a built-in family of stepsons twelve and sixteen. That would have been a major life change in peacetime, but this was wartime, when society was full of changes, uncertainties, and difficulties.

The man who became my stepfather on that June morning in 1942 was born on April 13 in 1904 in Cleveland, Oswego County, New York. He was the son of Charles Haynes and Elmina Eaton Haynes, and he had an older sister, Elma. The family lived in the small white farmhouse on the highway two miles east of Cleveland which was now to become my home. My stepfather's father was a glass cutter in one of the glass factories there in Cleveland. Almost no trace of the glass factories now remains, or none that I ever saw, but in the early years of the century, Cleveland made a great quantity of glass using the abundant sand close at hand. Years later, it became more sensible to ship the sand to where fuel was cheaper for the glassmaking process. As far as Cleveland was concerned, that turned out to be a hundred miles or more south in Pennsylvania. For my stepfather's father and others in Cleveland, that meant moving south to mills in places like Kane, Pennsylvania, and Clarksburg, West Virginia.

It's easy to talk about individuals pulling themselves up by their own bootstraps. Usually this means making their way from poverty to prosperity against the odds. But as I learned more about my stepfather, I understood poignantly well that the obstacles are not only financial but emotional. In the end, Charlie Haynes triumphed over troubles that I think would have stopped many a lesser man.

On his thirteenth birthday, which fell on Friday the thirteenth that year, he came home from school in Cleveland to find that his mother had hanged herself. His sister, Elma, was sent to live with relatives. My stepfather and his father stayed on in the farmhouse, although it was also the beginning of a somewhat peripatetic life, in which father and son moved alternately between the glass mills in the mid-South and back to the farm in Cleveland. His father took his son down to Kane, Pennsylvania, to find work in the glass factories there. For a while, the Hayneses lived in a hotel in Kane, and my stepfather was haunted for years afterward by memories of a fire in the hotel. Ever after, his first move in any hotel was to locate the fire escape. According to his obituary in the *National Glass Budget*, a trade paper, the elder Haynes was actually, for a time, a union organizer and developed a reputation not as a firebrand but as a dedicated and admired man of principle. In 1931 he was president of the Window Glass Cutters and Flatteners Protective Association of America.

My stepfather, a bright and precocious student, graduated from high school in Cleveland when he was still only sixteen. Young Harold Haynes, as he was known around Cleveland to distinguish him from his father, went to Hobart College in Geneva, with the help, I think, of the local Episcopal priest, George MacNish, whom I was to meet much later. After graduation and—I now speculate—although still too young emotionally for the rigors of attending the Harvard Business School, he did begin studies there beside the

Charles River. But the pressure was too great and he dropped out, something I feel he always regretted. He went to New York and got a job as a claims adjuster for an insurance company. He told me he hated the work.

He was, it's now easy for me to believe, a man with heavy burdens deriving from his mother's suicide, prey to the periods of depression that were to challenge him all his life. By his own admission, he became an alcoholic, who kept body and soul together after a fashion as a day laborer, topping onions in the vast fields at Canastota, New York, and in winter shoveling snow in the New York Central Railroad yards in Syracuse. At some point in the early 1930s, he bottomed out, took hold of his life, and began the slow, hard climb back up to respectability, sobriety and success that would have seemed to have been his future when he was a bright young man at Hobart. Like many another young man in the 1930s, he owed a debt to the New Deal. He became a timekeeper for the WPA (Works Progress Administration) and was assigned to a bridge-building project over the southern inlet to Keuka Lake at Hammondsport.

He rented a room at the home of James Smellie, one of the town's two pharmacists and, as the fates decreed it, a former high school classmate of my mother's. And so was set in motion events that would in time affect my life and my brother Joe's and, of course, our mother's. Charlie Haynes and my mother met casually as mutual friends of Jim Smellie. At that time my parents were divorced, which meant that Mother, a good and observant Catholic, could not remarry. My father remarried and slipped further from my life. He died at only forty-six on Christmas Day, 1938.

As the worst of the Depression began to ease, my stepfather took the bold decision of going into business for himself. He launched Charles H. Haynes, Inc., which specialized in selling obscure but vital devices used in cement construction on roads, bridges, dams, and buildings. I was soon to learn the names of these strange things—snap ties, screw anchors, lag studs, tie screws—mostly made by an outfit down in Brooklyn. I could never identify one piece from another, although I at various times lugged bags or boxes of the stuff into the trunk of the car for emergency delivery to construction sites.

My stepfather was by definition a traveling salesman, whose territory covered much of the center slice of the state, from the Pennsylvania border to the Canadian border and running as far west as Lake Erie. His travels, by accident or intent, took him to Hammondsport and I became used to his occasional, lightning visits, driving most often in a succession of Ford coupes. He was also an inveterate letter writer. In those Hammondsport days, I'd fetched the mail from Box 175 at the post office and grown used to seeing my future stepfather's sprawling hand on the envelopes, or his idiosyncratic typing, which allowed no spaces after initials or numbers, as if it were necessary to conserve room. He sent recipes, newspaper clippings, magazine articles in a steady flow.

I suppose I was quite naïve. I'd become accustomed to our being a single-parent family, just the three of us, though with a large population of aunts, uncles, great aunts, and great uncles within walking distance. I had no idea that I was a sort of postal go-between for a courtship in progress. I'm not even sure that it seemed like a courtship to Mother, although, in time, obviously something more was afoot than friendship.

He was round-faced and ruddy, sturdy but not fat. His hands, I was always surprised to notice, were rather small. He was a great asker of questions and a great listener. He had a broad, quick smile and a laugh that always seemed surprising because he was then and always essentially serious. But when he did laugh, it trailed off into a kind of head-shaking "Wow" that suggested he thought it was unusual that anything could be so funny.

He wore gray pin-striped suits and blue button-down shirts, all from Brooks Brothers, I'm sure. And one black knit tie, which seemed to grow longer each year and was a kind of good luck charm. In season, he wore a straw hat—also, I think, from Brooks—with the brim turned up all round, and a fedora in winter.

Early in 1941, my stepfather's father came home to Cleveland from Clarksburg, West Virginia, where he'd been working as a glass cutter. He died suddenly in April and, at that point, it's clear that Charlie Haynes felt he was free to ask Mother to marry him. In theory at least, he was in the peculiar position of needing not only Mother's consent, but Joe's and mine as well. But we of course gave our consent eagerly because it was quite obviously the decision Mother hoped for.

I knew that Mother had married a kind, wonderfully curious, endlessly hardworking man, tentative rather than in any way controlling so far as Joe and I were concerned. Mother was still in charge of us. The habit was hard to break. Perhaps the largest part of the new chapter that was opening in our lives was learning just how remarkable our stepfather was.

Settling In

The farmhouse where my stepfather and his father had lived as bachelors until his father died in 1941 had changed very little over the decades since it was built, sometime late in the nineteenth century. A stove in the middle of the living room had been the principal source of heat and the facilities were rudimentary. The two men had used only part of the house, which was now long unaccustomed to a population of four.

But my stepfather had worked miracles to get it ready for us. Fred Wise, the local carpenter, a craftsman of the old school, had done over the kitchen, modernized a downstairs bathroom, made another one upstairs, and renewed most of the floors, all in record time. The stairs to the second floor, where Fred had created two bedrooms beneath the sloping roof for Joe and me, still reflected the age of the farmhouse, with risers of different heights and steps of varying depth, so that going to bed was not without peril.

When my grandmother and I arrived, the place was still aswarm with activity. A new furnace had been installed in the deepened cellar. It was wood burning in view of likely wartime shortages of coal or heating oil. A local jack-of-all-trades named Grove Brockway and his sons had come to build a chimney for the furnace, a thing of beauty with gentle curves where you'd expect sharp angles. The Brockways all used language, quite unself-consciously, that would

CLEVELAND HOUSE: *The Haynes house east of Cleveland on the north shore of Oneida Lake dates from the mid–nineteenth century. The people on the porch may be my stepfather's parents. My stepfather was born here. The house looked the same when Mother, Joe, and I moved here in 1942, after she and Pop married. Courtesy Debbie Fisher.*

have got my mouth washed out with soap ten times a day. They seemed unaware of the occasionally appalled expressions on my grandmother's face, and less often on Mother's. For her, I think the soundtrack simply went with the adventure. She had, of course, left her whole past behind her, and hers had been troubled, whereas mine had really not been. Now she looked to the future with great excitement and she was in love.

To feed the furnace, logs were hauled in by a team of horses from the woodlots that stretched north from the house; they lay waiting to be cut, split, and stacked. I did a little splitting when nobody was around to see my ineptness. But everyone agreed, stacking was what I did best.

I would occasionally walk up in the woods and exorcise the pangs I felt about leaving Hammondsport. On the other hand, listening to the Brockways cuss each other out, as in some upcountry version of *Tobacco Road*, I began to see the value for the would-be writer of this colorful new experience.

My stepfather's sister, Elma, and some other family members called my stepfather "Duke" for reasons I never knew. Joe and I decided that "Duke" and "Charlie" and "Father" and "Dad" were all inappropriate, so we agreed to call him "Pop." If he minded, he never said so. (For a long time, I thought it was only the best of unsatisfactory choices, and even found it a little patronizing, yet over the years, "Pop" grew on all of us.)

Battening down the hatches for the long war took several forms, one at least bordering on farce. Through George Kaiser, the local butcher, Pop bought half a hog, some of which George cut up for freezing, but with a considerable number of other mysterious pieces, which could only be ground up for sausage. Looking back, I find it almost miraculous that Mother remained a meat eater after being elbow-deep in hog fat for days on end.

At the same time, my grandmother thought it would be prudent

to put up some cucumber pickles she called her "nine-day won-
ders." They actually did require soaking in crocks of brine for nine
days, with the brine changed daily. The pungent aroma, hinting of
the seashore on a particularly hot and brackish day, filled the house,
but I must say that, in the end, the pickles were worth the trouble,
and so was the pork sausage.

Huckleberries grew in great abundance in the swampy woodlot
north of the house. The Brockway women showed up to pick the
berries and Joe and I joined them. Mother canned whole shelves full
of them as well. They contributed to wonderful pies, muffins, and
bread.

In due time, our furniture arrived from Hammondsport. The
most important item for me was my grandfather Masson's turn-of-
the-century rolltop desk. It was and still is a heavy brute made of
solid oak, and while the upper part, the rolltop, is separate from the
bottom part, the drawers, I still don't know how we ever got the desk
up those medieval steps to the front bedroom, which was mine. But
with many hands sharing the burden, it did get there and it snuggled
nicely against the sloping roof. I'd felt for years reassured as a potential writer by the possession of that desk, with all of its slots and
cubbyholes and an assortment of wonderful drawers, and the
matching heavy oak swivel chair. Once in Cleveland, the desk became a symbol of my former life and my future one. There under the
eaves, I would sit at the desk and look out the window toward the
lake and dream of being a writer. I still have the desk and use it and
it still confirms to me that I am a writer, although the present tools of
my trade—computer, copier, printer, fax machine—line the opposite
side of my office.

In those first weeks at Cleveland, Pop was, I'm sure, studying us
to see what kind of stepsons he was now responsible for. For myself,
I became aware later rather than at the time that I was studying Pop,
too, discovering the personality of the man mother had married.

ROLLTOP DESK: *The rolltop desk had been my grandfather's and came to us in Cleveland from Hammondsport. Even as a teenager, I felt it confirmed my status as a potential writer. Photo by Peggy Champlin.*

What struck me first was that some of the habits of his bachelor years had stayed with him. His favorite meal was slices of bread crumbled into a bowl of milk. I think he'd learned over the years that it sometimes deflected the migraine headaches he could sense coming on. He ran on a high quotient of nervous energy. To Mother's detectable but unexpressed dismay, he would sometimes opt for bread and milk instead of what she'd carefully prepared.

If bread and milk was a legacy of his earlier years, so was eating at furious speed and getting back to the office or his reading. He would be finished before the rest of us had much more than touched our plates. He would sit there patiently but obviously eager to get away. Mother would usually suggest quietly that he get on with his work and he would leave the table gratefully.

He had no great mechanical gifts and an impatience with mechanical things, especially those which didn't work. He paid $12.50 for the very first ballpoint pen. After a trial, he announced sardonically that it really was a wonder: it would make nineteen carbon copies—and no original. When the ignition key froze in the lock on one of his Fords, Harold Morse came out and installed a new ignition switch. Pop took the old one, with the key still locked in the lock, and threw it across the field. Only then did he remember that the old key worked the doors and the trunk, and the new ignition key wouldn't. The three of us spent a couple of hours searching the field, high with weeds, until we found the damned thing.

Pop had many qualities that I admired and that attracted me, but, above all, he was one of the most insatiably and intellectually curious men I've ever known, and one of the most eclectic readers. Joe remembers that he subscribed to forty magazines. I'm not sure it was quite that many, but the list ran from *Engineering News-Record* and other specialized construction periodicals to *Farm Journal, Vermont Life, Time, Fortune,* the *New Yorker,* and two daily newspapers. He was fascinated by the business of business, by the rich, by successful executives, and by the tales of the old, rich families, including the descendants of the robber barons from the nineteenth century. He had what seemed to me to be total recall of family connections and corporate histories. He was far from uncritical about the sleazy successes and the scions who gambled away family fortunes. He was a moralist in business, which was one of the sides of him I came to appreciate. Ingenuity he admired; sharp practice he did not. One whole wall of the living room was bookshelves, and one of the books he returned to regularly was *A History of the Businessman*, a study going back to medieval times.

He read deeply about Stonewall Jackson, Robert E. Lee, and dozens of other generals on both sides of the Civil War. He read left-wing novels by Louis Aragon (although Pop was a Republican, narrowly) and Edmund Wilson's *Memoirs of Hecate County*. He was—and I became—a great admirer of Walter D. Edmonds and his historical novels set in the very country where we were living. There were books not only on the shelves but on almost every flat surface in the house. It was a reader's dream; I felt I was in heaven. I was reading beyond my years, of course, and I think Mother might have been shocked at some of my exposures to the sexier side of life in Wilson's book and others.

I don't know that I had any serious thoughts then about becoming a journalist; I wanted to—had to—write, that's all I knew. But I could have deciphered the signs if I'd wanted to, in my love of newspapers and magazines. The *New York Herald-Tribune* (that lovely, doomed journal) arrived every day, and I plowed through the military solemnities of Major George Fielding Eliot and the graceful profundities of Walter Lippmann, and, more to my point, the lively drama criticism of Walter Kerr.

"There's a divinity that shapes our ends, rough-hew them how we will," Shakespeare wrote. Looking back, I know how profoundly true that is, but in the late summer of 1942, I had no way of foreseeing how my future would be hewn.

Discovering Cleveland, New York

W hen our bikes arrived from Hammondsport at last, Joe and I used to ride into town, curious to know a little bit more about the place where we now lived. We found that there was a swimming hole just north of the village in an abandoned sand mine.

Slowly I came to know a few of the adults in Cleveland. There was George Kaiser, the quiet-voiced and laconic butcher who lived over his shop and who, so far as I could tell, had no life outside the shop, although this was almost certainly not so. The Apps were the primary mercantile family in town. One of them ran the boat livery, and two sisters ran a sort of all-purpose shop in their house next to George's butcher shop. We stopped there on Sundays to buy the Syracuse and Utica papers. For no rational reason, I always felt uneasy in their presence, and I initially felt that they were subjecting Joe and me, along with Mother, to intense scrutiny as the threesome who had disrupted the calm tenor of local life, and about whom little was known. I do them a posthumous injustice; in time, the three of us were well accepted in Cleveland. But I think it was also true that Pop may have courted one of the App cousins and that, as a bachelor in his late thirties, he had undoubtedly shocked the town by marrying a widow with two half-grown boys. The App ladies had a nephew who lived on Fifth Avenue in New York and who was later in my class at Harvard, but I think Cleveland and Fifth Avenue seemed as inconceivably far removed for him as they did for me; we saw very little of each other, and even then accidentally.

On the other side of George Kaiser's meat market was the most important establishment in those wartime years, Morse's garage. Morse's kept Pop's succession of Fords running, which became increasingly important as time went by; he also watched over my grandmother's Buick when she came to Cleveland to live in 1947. The garage looked like the set for a period movie in a small town. You could imagine Humphrey Bogart as a gangster on the lam, roaring up in a desperate hurry to get some gas.

One of the first people we got to know in town was Marvin Brown, the village doctor, who took wonderful and compassionate care of my grandmother in her last, failing years, and then of Mother when she began her eighteen-year battle with cancer.

The one local celebrity, my stepfather told me, was Lou Gregory, the high school coach, who each year went off to run in the Boston Marathon and always did well. The town's Catholic priest, Father John Butler, was what American priests now occasionally refer to as one of the "FBI"—foreign-born Irish. He was ascetic looking, with a rather high and liquid voice, and he'd brought with him all the Irish dislike, bordering on hatred, of the English. Even during the war, his sermons were as apt to be diatribes against Winston Churchill as homilies on the miracle of loaves and fishes. Most significantly in the life of our family, he was an early mentor to Joe on his journey to the priesthood. He was also kindly attentive to Mother during her illness, even after he'd retired to a residence for elderly priests in Syracuse. So saying, I have to confess my sharpest memories are of sermons that seemed to me overly long and ill-advised, especially his harangues against those who did not attend Mass—directed, inevitably, at a congregation of those who did. In later years, one of Joe's other priest friends told him, "Joe, just remember you don't save any souls after the first five minutes." Father Butler would have disagreed.

My stepfather was an Episcopalian, conscientious and observant. That brought us into frequent contact with the Episcopal priest, a wonderful eccentric named George MacNish. Mac, as he was known to all, was a tall, rugged, but slightly stooped figure who must have been in his sixties when we first knew him. He had a deep and resonant voice and was keen on the ideas of physical fitness, courage, and military readiness. His great hero was General George Patton. One of his proudest moments was getting a letter published in *Time*, defending Patton from someone's complaint that the general had invoked God's name to get good weather before a battle. "Patton got his weather, he won his fight," MacNish wrote, loyal both to the general and to God. Despite his stand on fitness, he smoked, seldom removing his cigarette from his lips, so that there was usually a gray chain of ashes down the front of the shirts or cardigans he wore. He lived in a small cabin in a grove of trees on a cliff at the water's edge, just east of town. I envied him then, and it still seems like the perfect setting for a writer. Mac indeed used to write and self-publish pamphlets on his favorite subjects. He was also a golfer, who, I believe, owned the local links for some years, and he was a walker, who would show up unannounced at the house, having walked out from town. He would treat us to a small lecture on the progress of the war, sip a glass of wine or a cup of tea, and occasionally consent to be driven back to town.

Now and again, I've wished I'd been a few years older so I could have conversed more easily and come to know better some of the figures in my young life. MacNish was one of them. I was just a shade too young to have asked him some of the questions I should have (or perhaps those I think of only now)—about his faith, about his early life, about his life then in 1942, about the dreams he'd had and perhaps had lost, or the serenity he'd come to. He was one of those true originals, the country pastor of a kind more celebrated in England than here, whose relationship to God and to his small congregation, though surely unorthodox, was nonetheless shepherd-like in its own way. But, as with your own relatives, by the time you even know the questions you want to ask, it is much too late to ask them.

There are many questions I wish I'd known to ask Pop, but I have to be content with the memories of those days and our time together at the farmhouse.

Joe

My brother, Joseph Masson Champlin, was born on May 11, 1930. That made him my kid brother by four years, an almost uncrossable gap when he is two and you are six—and even when he is six and you are ten. It took years—sometimes painful years—before we were truly brothers and we forgot about the time gap between us. We have always loved each other, but there have been occasional failures of communication. It remains true that being a kid brother is an awful fate, particularly in those years when the older brother is himself just barely into his teens, and wants to pal around with his contemporaries and not with his kid brother. I am afraid I gave Joe, or "Jo-Jo," as he was known in the Hammondsport years, quite a bad time. He has subsequently made a magnificent recovery, which is the story of his life, and I am now known as Joe's brother and my role as his older brother is much diminished.

When we were very young, our mother used to serve us supper on trays in the living room so that we could listen to "Little Orphan Annie" and "Tom Mix" and "The Ralston Straight-Shooters" and a couple of other serials on the radio. I have two special memories of those days. The most embarrassing and painful is of an afternoon when, for reasons I no longer remember, I got mad at Joe and pushed his chair over backward with him in it. He could have been hurt but luckily he wasn't. He didn't even cry much because, as I realized later, he did very little crying as a child. The other memory I keep vividly in mind was an afternoon when Joe couldn't finish his supper. It may have been a tuna fish casserole—all his life Joe has had a distaste bordering on revulsion for fish in any form. This made meal planning difficult before the Church lifted its ban on eating meat on Friday. Joe is as anti-fish as he is pro what he calls "PB&Js," or peanut butter and jelly sandwiches. He stared at the unconsumed tuna casserole and, for once, he cried silently, tears welling up in his eyes. "People in China," Joe said, "don't have enough to eat." He was ashamed of being unable to finish his dinner, the more so as he thought of the starving millions in China. A Sunday or two earlier, I think, we'd had a particularly fiery and outspoken missionary give a guest sermon up at St. Gabriel's Church. And the missionary's vivid descriptions of famine had obviously affected Joe deeply.

Though he can't have been more than six years old, Joe's tears spoke eloquently of a sensitivity I found touching, and I was vaguely ashamed that I'd not responded the same way myself. Not that I thought Joe was bound for the priesthood, but looking back years later, I would always recall that evening in the living room with the radio playing and the casserole uneaten.

Also in later years, I was struck by the way Joe and I seemed to confirm some sort of genetic laws governing inherited traits. Joe had the kind of dark brown eyes teenage girls found incredibly romantic and a full head of dark brown hair. He absolutely resembled Mother in his coloring. I inherited our father's coloring, with hazel eyes and hair of a much lighter brown. It used to be brown anyway, but at least I still have it, which is more than Joe can say. Joe has evidently inherited hair loss from our father, who was largely bald by his early thirties.

Joe wrote left-handed as soon as he was able to write, and he still does, in a small and frequently indecipherable script. Although we both threw baseballs left-handed, I have always written right-handed, probably because of the stern influence of my first grade teacher, Miss Nina Arland. Miss Arland's brother, who worked for New York Telephone, had told her that the company simply wouldn't hire left-handed persons. The thought that none of us would ever be able to work for the phone company if we were left-handed was appalling to her. I think Miss Arland had retired by the time Joe came along.

Joe inherited all the athletic ability in the family. Which side of the family those skills descended from I don't know. I think our father played rugby at his prep school in Canada but, after that, I think he and athletics were strangers. Though Joe played soccer at Yale, his favorite sport was baseball. Against all conventional wisdom, he was a left-handed catcher. I don't think there is a left-handed catcher in the major leagues today, and I don't know that there was ever one in the past.

I was an altar boy at an early age and I was a good and faithful one. Occasionally I would be excused from school to ride with the priest over the hills to Prattsburg, which had no resident priest, to serve at a midweek funeral. Now Hammondsport has no resident priest either, but is visited once a month or so by a priest who functions like a circuit preacher. Joe was an altar boy, too. Although Dick Lanpher and I were the principal servers, on Sundays, four younger, shorter boys knelt at the sides of the altar and Joe was one of those, along with Justin Berlureau and the two Grimaldi boys.

At what point it began to be clear that Joe had a vocation for the priesthood I really don't know. Father John Butler, the pastor at St. Mary's in Cleveland, said that he detected in the sensitivity of Joe's confessions that he had the makings of a priest—this, when Joe was twelve years old. Although he and I have never really discussed it, I sense that Joe put himself to the test to be absolutely sure that the priesthood was where he wanted to spend the rest of his life. He tested himself by enjoying the secular life. He dated in high school,

JOE THROWING BASEBALL: *Catchers were never left-handed, but Joe was, as seen here in the side yard in Cleveland in about 1942. He was the family athlete and a very skillful one, too.*

as absolutely innocently as everybody dated in high school in those days, and he dated some of the outstanding young women of his class. Years later, he would baptize some of their children. He played three high school sports and was captain of the baseball team.

He was famous around Hammondsport as a very young child for his devotion to the Bath and Hammondsport Railroad. He persuaded Mother to buy him a full-sized lunch bucket and trainman's cap, jacket, and trousers, intended for play-acting of course, but which he wore every Saturday down to the depot where he spent the day riding the B&H the eight miles south to Bath and back again at a steady ten miles an hour. The station agent kept in the office safe for years a small notebook in which Joe had recorded the serial numbers of every boxcar the B&H had hauled on his working days. In his first two college years, with his love of railroads still intact, Joe worked on the track gang of the New York, Ontario and Western Railroad, which ran past our house at Cleveland. It was terrific exercise, although he suffered horrendously from poison ivy and his skin was often bright red from neck to toe. In his freshman year at Yale, he got a part-time job for a professor who was researching a railroad project. It was a glorious assignment.

But the joys of dating and the challenges of an excellent prep school, Andover, and a storied Ivy League college only confirmed Joe's conviction that his future lay elsewhere.

After his freshman year at Yale, he transferred to Notre Dame, where he took courses in preparation for entering St. Bernard's Seminary, near Rochester, New York. Most summers during his five years at the seminary, he worked for our ailing stepfather in his construction supplies business. Joe drove as many as two thousand miles a week, visiting bridge- and road-building sites. The experience proved invaluable in later years when he was running parishes and needed to know about balance sheets and other exotic business matters. He was ordained in February 1956.

At some point early on, he had seriously considered joining the Trappist Order, essentially withdrawing from the world for a life of silence, contemplation, prayer, and good works like baking bread to support the monastery. He visited the monastery at Geneseo, New York, several times. But our Mother, who was as devout a Catholic as I've ever known, drew the line at the monastic idea. She argued from a position of absolute wisdom that someone with Joe's kind and outgoing personality had a far more important contribution to make in the real world. Joe perceived soon enough that she was right. I suspect that he'd gone through a phase that many young men and women go through, seeing the romantic side of giving oneself to God. I've often felt that many a young man has been all but hypnotized by the rituals, the purity, the fineness of the priestly life, only to discover a decade or two later that the demands of celibacy are severe indeed, and finally unbearable. For a while in my early days in Los Angeles, I would often hear from fine young men who, having been seminary classmates of Joe's or working colleagues in the diocese, had left their priestly calling, perhaps married, and were making new lives for themselves in the secular world. I found it hard not to feel a real pang of sympathy for these men who had committed years of their lives to a demanding dream and found that they couldn't sustain it—or that it couldn't sustain them. At the same time, as the years went by, I came more and more to admire what I have always described as Joe's serenity, a serenity achieved in unending struggle against all the temptations of the world, including, far from least, the joys of love and family and parenthood. To remain celibate within the secular world is nothing less than heroic. I think finally that only a supreme identification with the love of God and the serenity that comes with the assurance of that love will suffice.

Joe has brought to his priesthood of more than a half century not only a sublime faith but a wonderful sense of humor and the ability to deal shrewdly with the real world and its all too imperfect people.

His first parish after various other assignments was at Holy Family in Fulton, New York, where he also developed a reputation as a long-distance runner. Indeed, he later ran a marathon in Canada. His friends at a subsequent parish gave him a sweatshirt for the event. On the front, it said, "Father Champlin, Camillus, New York," and on the back, "Confessions later, follow me." Assigned to the Church's North American College in Rome, where he lectured on pastoral duties, he was perhaps the only American to return from a year in Italy having lost ten pounds.

Early in his priesthood, Joe began to write and publish voluminously. He has in fact become the far more prolific writer of the two of us, with something like fifty volumes published and over twenty million copies sold. His first best seller was a softcover book aimed at teenagers entitled *Don't You Really Love Me?* Its theme was that chastity in the long run is more comfortable and far more trouble-free than sexual freedom. Not long after the book came out, Joe was invited to speak to the Archdiocesan Council of Catholic Women in Los Angeles. He was introduced by an ancient Irish monsignor who had obviously never heard of him but said it was nice he'd chosen for his title "those dear words of Our Lord to us all, 'Don't you really love me?' " At the end of the talk, however, the monsignor confided to the woman who ran the council how upset he was that Father Champlin had not once used the word "sin." "Monsignor," the wise lady said, "if Father Champlin had used the word 'sin,' every teenager in the audience would have turned him off like a radio." As it was, there was a line of two dozen teenagers waiting to speak with Joe after the talk.

Joe later wrote *Together for Life,* a guide to help engaged couples build their own wedding ceremony with readings of their own choice. Often presented to couples when they begin their marriage preparation with the priest, it remains a phenomenal best seller; as of this writing, sales have exceeded nine million copies.

For a time, Joe also wrote a column that appeared in diocesan newspapers. In one column, he acknowledged a growing demand among Catholic laypeople for more dialogue in the operation of the Church. For his pains, his column was yanked from the diocesan paper in Syracuse and he was removed from several posts.

For ten years, Joe was the much-loved rector of the Cathedral of the Immaculate Conception in Syracuse. In 2005, at the age of seventy-five, he left the Cathedral for a small parish near Syracuse, where he lives in the rectory. These days, he is freed of most administrative chores but still is kept busy saying Mass and performing weddings, often of those he'd baptized years before, as well as baptisms and other pastoral duties.

While at the Cathedral, he launched what he called his "Guardian Angel Society" to build an endowment for scholarships to help students, mostly black and nearly all living well below the poverty line, to attend the Cathedral elementary school and to go on to the Catholic junior and senior high schools, which must charge tuition. He has raised more than a million dollars. For several years, he ran a 5K race, betting his parishioners that he would finish within a certain time. If he did, he collected the bets; if not, he returned the money. It was a safe bet for him. In 2001 alone, his run raised more than $50,000 for the Guardian Angel Society. The Cathedral, like most cathedrals deep in the inner city, has its inevitable problems, although few as startling as the afternoon he and the custodian found a street person taking a bath in the baptistry.

For many years, Joe traveled widely, giving Church missions, talking to the priests in several dioceses, and lecturing on ways to energize parishes. He has even been summoned to South America to talk at seminars, exploring ways to revitalize the Church there. We are as close as two brothers can be and he is a superb uncle and grand-uncle several times over.

In 2000, Joe was bothered by a persistent hacking cough. Tests showed that he had an obscure form of cancer that the doctors say is treatable but not curable. His treatment involves regular chemotherapy, which in its first months was devastatingly hard on Joe. More recently, his body has seemed to tolerate it a bit better. Having been, as he said, a "sick puppy" in the early stages, he now seems to be over the worst of it, regaining much of the weight, and much of the energy, he lost. He has recently started to run the four-mile run he used to do regularly. He has also been swimming a half mile a day in Skaneateles Lake, where he has a summer cottage. He is, as he has been from his early adolescent years, a model of enviable serenity. He knew early on that he had a vocation, a calling to devote his life to the love and service of God. He has never regretted the choice.

Camden, New York

The Cleveland house was almost on the dividing line between Oswego and Oneida Counties. For business reasons, Pop used Oswego County as part of his mailing address. But there was a larger, better school twelve miles north in the village of Camden in Oneida County. Pop persuaded the Camden officials to let Joe and me attend Camden Central School.

On a lovely, late summer day in August, Mother drove us over to Camden to enroll. About two miles east on Route 49 (a stretch of road Joe and I would get to know very well) was the tiny hamlet of Jewell, sometimes called "West Vienna" (pronounced "vyENa"). There a narrow, two-lane macadam road led north from Route 49 toward Camden. Just above Route 49, beyond a large pond created by a small dam, was an old, but still-tended cemetery, where some of my stepfather's ancestors were buried.

The road twisted and turned uphill through a piney woods, then curved down and crossed a small stream. The dappled light through the trees gave the scene a timeless quality, as if it might all have looked much the same long before there were cars and macadam.

Emerging from the woods, the road climbed steeply to the crest of a hill and then dropped even more sharply down into Camden, which sits essentially in a bowl of hills. Its major business, even now, is making wire, and in that summer of 1942, the mill was already

32

working around the clock on production for the war effort. There was also in town a prosperous local firm that sold stamps to beginning philatelists and another that printed collection envelopes for churches.

We found our way to the school, where I was interviewed by the principal, Donald H. Barker, a man who was to have as much bearing on the rest of my life as anyone outside my family. Don Barker was an imposing figure, with sharp blue eyes and a hawk-like nose, but his voice was quiet, well-modulated, and gentle, almost feminine. There was then, and perhaps still is, something de-genderizing about public education, probably more so a half century ago, when teachers and principals were hardly thought to have private lives, let alone sexual identities. Barker's voice conveyed a kind of steady neutrality, although it could suddenly turn cold and stern when discipline demanded it. He was a superior school administrator. I kept in touch with him for years afterward when he was in retirement in Florida, and with his widow and son after he died.

Looking over my transcript from Hammondsport, Barker noted that, in addition to a full course load, I had credits for extracurricular activities like band, glee club, and sports (junior varsity basketball was the summit of my skills). With all my credits, he said, and if I could handle two years of English at once, I could telescope my junior and senior years into one and graduate in June 1943, when I would still be seventeen, instead of June 1944, when I would be eighteen and exceedingly draftable. It meant the possibility of at least a taste of college before I went into service. And since I had no vision of myself, even then, except as a writer—some kind of a writer—two years of English in one sounded like pleasure, not pain. By such small deflections are whole lives changed.

The cheerful interview with Barker meant that I did get to college. It affected my choice of college, and the choice of college bore directly on the job that determined my whole career. None of that was foreseeable, of course, on a warm August afternoon; as it turned out, there were a few adventures to be had in the meantime.

Getting to school in Camden from Cleveland was itself an adventure, enjoyable in the warm days of Indian summer, when brother Joe and I could ride our bikes the mile and a half east on 49 and park them in LeGrand Salem's barn at Jewell. We waited at the junction for Rose Sable to gather us up in her station wagon, which was our bus to Camden. Rose, who lived up the road in North Bay, always played the radio at high volume (on cold days it seemed to add a little warmth). Her Syracuse station of choice featured what would now be called a morning drive show, with a small musical group and an emcee named Fred Jeske. Disc jockeys hadn't yet won the day. Jeske had a deep voice and played the piano, running a five-note motif and spelling out his name, J-E-S-K-E. The band's one tune that survives in memory, the underscoring for those early morning rides over the hill, is "It's a Long Way to Tipperary." From the depths of memory come the vague faces of the other riders: those of Shirley Perkins, who later worked for the phone company in Syracuse, of Dorcas Kirk and her two brothers, and of one or two others. Most of the time, we all smelled of wet wool from rain or melting snow.

Camden is two or three times the size of Hammondsport. The school was centralized, with a huge fleet of buses carrying the kids from and to Taberg, McConnellsville, North Bay, Vienna, Osceola, Blossvale, Redfield, Fish Creek, Florence, and the other outlying towns. The first few days, the size of the school and the sea of new faces were intimidating. So was having to get on the bus. But it didn't take long to discover that Camden Central School had its share of pretty girls, which did much to relieve the pain of leaving Hammondsport.

On the other hand, I was now a bus person, not a local. This was an inconvenience—no extracurricular activities. And the school had a dance band, whose theme song was "Stairway to the Stars," played slowly and majestically. The song is another evocative link to my Camden year. I would have given anything to play in a dance band, but I realized both that I couldn't make rehearsals and that the trumpet players were much better than I was anyway.

Being a bus rider struck me as diminishing my status. The town kids had always been a sort of elite in Hammondsport, and I anticipated it would be so in Camden, too. Camden had a high percentage of commuting students, and the townies didn't seem to be quite so dominant in school affairs as they'd been in Hammondsport. But Howie Hornung, whose father ran the local news shop and pool hall, and George Carle, whose father ran the tombstone business, were the big men in the class.

The big women on campus (not physically, I'm glad to say) were Marje Walton and Jean Bradley, both minister's daughters, and Fern Adsit, whose father clerked in the post office. Marje became a lifelong friend and, a few years later, she and my wife-to-be roomed together in Albany, where they were both working. Jean was a gifted actress, and her reading of Dorothy Parker's monologue "The Waltz" made one assembly wonderfully hilarious. I have often wondered whether Jean was able to make a career in theater. Fern was petite and beautiful and we went steady for a long time. She eventually became a nurse and married a doctor.

As I used to do in Hammondsport, I wore a sport coat and necktie to school every day—the better to conceal my scrawniness. But I realized soon enough that the downside was that this made me look like a snob since flannel shirts and corduroys or jeans were, even then, the male costume of choice. But, in time, I acquired a secondary reputation for saying something funny once in a while and being friendly. The jacket and ties were, I guess, accepted as eccentricities.

I started writing for the school paper, which was called "Facts and Fizz" and occupied a full page once a month in the local weekly, the *Camden Advance-Journal.* The paper's editor and his wife, Walter and Florence Stone, became my friends and remained so long after I'd left Camden. My pieces were mostly hard-hitting editorials on the war effort—in favor of buying bonds and collecting scrap paper. I can't believe anyone read them. Florence Stone, who would write me letters into her nineties, was the liveliest, gossipiest, and most enchanting correspondent I ever had.

Then the Indian summer died, and it turned cold. In the foothills of the Adirondacks, where Camden is, snow, icy winds, more snow, and subzero temperatures are lurking in the wings by Labor Day and waste little time coming on stage. By November, there was snow on the road, so the bikes were useless, and Joe and I were trudging along Route 49 to Jewell by the first, thin light of day. And almost every day, the wind whistled off Oneida Lake unrelentingly. We bent into the wind and the scarves across our faces would be covered with frost by the time we got to the bus stop, where we stood stomping to get some feeling back into our feet.

One of the mottoes that loom large in my life is "I can take suffering or leave it alone." It was unthinkable, but I began to ponder how I could stay in Camden and not have to take the bus. The walk to and from the bus was a nuisance and often painful, and with wartime rationing and Pop's new job in a war plant there were no lifts to the bus stop for us. I was missing out on much of the life of the school.

I decided to do something about it. A classmate of mine told me that the local restaurant needed a dishwasher. My classmate was a short-order cook at the place. The restaurant was called the "D&C," for D-something and Carpenter. One noon hour, I dashed to the D&C, and proprietor Bud Carpenter said he would be delighted to have me wash dishes for him at thirty-five cents an hour. The next day, I called at 111 Main Street, a three-story frame house where Mrs. Labby took boarders. She said she had a large back room that contained a cot and a double bed. "In summers," Mrs. Labby said, "there's drummers, salesmen, you know, who rent the double bed but they don't come in winter and I can let you have the cot for five dollars a week. Just so you know there might be times when I have to rent the double bed." Now I had a job and a place to lay my head. All I had to do was tell Mother.

I knew what a shock to the system these tidings would be for her and, several children of my own later, I'm still more aware of the specters of danger, corruption, and disaster that must have risen before her, even though I would be only twelve miles over the hill. I didn't think she would go along with my plan, but she did and the job became, with all else, a symbol of a new and independent life.

I realized with an embarrassed concern that this left Joe, now in junior high, to make the commute to the bus at Jewell all by himself in all weathers. I've never found ways to apologize adequately for abandoning him, although he has never complained.

I was ever more convinced that, one way or another, I was going to become a writer. As I sat in my room in the boardinghouse, which included a kind of vanity bureau of tall oak and an almost full-length mirror, I felt very much like a romantic hero facing the world alone. God, it was melodramatic. We had worked out a system by which Mrs. Labby at eight every morning banged on the steam pipe in the kitchen. It ran up through my room and was an inescapable alarm clock.

My dishwashing chores started after school and I washed dishes until the restaurant closed at eleven. I was undoubtedly violating all manner of child labor laws. I'd freed myself from the captivity of the bus ride to the captivity of the kitchen sinks, where there was never enough hot water and where much of the time I was up to my elbows in the dirtiest dishwater I'd ever known. I did that six days a week, then caught a ride home to Cleveland at eleven o'clock Saturday night with a Cleveland man who worked at the Camden wire mill. The time card for my first week read "60.5 hours."

Noel Coward wrote in one of his plays, "Cheap music is so potent." It certainly is. I heard every record on the restaurant's jukebox dozens of times. And "Moonlight Becomes You," "Don't Get Around Much Anymore," and Glenn Miller's "Juke Box Saturday Night" will haunt me all my days, fetching me back to the D&C.

The pattern I attempted to follow was to dash to the boarding-house when I'd scoured the last pan, then sit in front of the mirror, the only place to put my books down, and stare at myself as I fought sleep and tried to study. Sleep always won. In the morning, I could stay awake in class, but after a good lunch in the school cafeteria, I couldn't stay awake in the afternoon. The chemistry teacher moved me to the very front seat and I would fall asleep staring at her.

I washed dishes through the holidays and into the new year. One Sunday when I was home, Mother said there was going to be a change. She'd called Don Barker at the high school when I started the job and asked him to warn her if my schoolwork seemed to be suffering. I might have known she would, but I thought it kind of Mr. Barker to wait as long as he did to sound the alarm. Mother and I reached a compromise. She generously said that I could continue to live at Mrs. Labby's boardinghouse. I said I would continue to wash dishes on Saturdays; it would almost pay the rent. Actually, I felt I'd learned as much as anyone ever needed to know about the art of washing dishes and I was delighted to go along with the plan.

I wasn't sorry to reduce my working hours—for a number of reasons. For one thing, Bud had brought on another dishwasher, a beefy wall-eyed French Canadian named Louie, who was, I think, only a point or two shy of being retarded. He had a fierce and irrational temper and, when things riled him, he threw cleavers and other handy objects around the kitchen.

One night before the new dispensation was in effect, I got home from the restaurant about midnight, dog-tired as usual. I dropped into bed and was instantly asleep. What seemed like minutes later, Mrs. Labby shook me awake and said in a quiet voice, "There's a blizzard."

It had been snowing when I went home. I murmured, "Yes."

"There's a couple here from Ilion and they can't get home. I rented them the double bed."

After telling me she'd taken my wallet out of my pants and put it under my pillow, she left. The couple didn't turn on the light but, in the darkness as I started to fall asleep again, there was the rustle of clothing being removed and then a woman's voice said, "Why, George, whoever thought I'd end up spending the night with you?" The virgin youth in the cot was suddenly bolt awake and only feigning sleep. The woman's whispered voice was saying, "George, stop, the kid. George, stop." I think I ruined it for George, but I fell asleep and cannot testify to the rest of the night. The next morning as I went off to work I glimpsed the couple paying Mrs. Labby in the kitchen. I saw them and they saw me and I saw that they weren't from Ilion at all, but were from Cleveland just over the hill. And I think they were a couple just for the convenience of the evening.

On Saturday, I helped out at the counter in the morning and the couple came in and sat where I would serve them. The man, who hadn't been able to shave, looked like an out-of-work lumberjack and he was scowling. He beckoned me to lean closer and he said, "Kid, you don't know anything." I shook my head and looked as dense as I could. I can't remember what they ordered.

It was, I thought, another chapter in the education of a young writer, although I never wrote about it until now, sixty years later. Had I ever had a hand for fiction, I could have used the boarding-house as the source for a whole series of stories—fictional, but inspired by a combination of observation and my occasionally feverish imagination.

There were two young women who worked at the wire mill and whom I found most attractive in a worldly way. But I felt they regarded me with the tolerant indifference reserved for kid brothers and nephews. The high school coach was another boarder while he waited to be called to active duty in the Navy. Many of my new high school pals were enlisting in various services as they turned eighteen. One night, six of us gathered at Mrs. Labby's to toast John Carpenter as he left for the Army. We had a quart of beer for the six of us. In those more innocent days, there wasn't much drinking in high school, certainly not at Camden. It was high spirits and not alcohol that made us noisy and silly. John fell into the bathtub, which was dry, and had a devil of a time getting out. The laughter roused Mrs. Labby, who was a pillar of the Women's Christian Temperance Union and was outraged. The coach had come along to see what was happening; most of his basketball team was represented. The next day, Mrs. Labby was on the phone to Don Barker, demanding that the coach be fired and the boys be expelled from school. Barker's gifts of diplomacy were equal to the task and nothing happened to any of us. Carpenter came back after the war to a nice career as a singer-actor on Broadway, including a principal role in the successful revival of *Guys and Dolls* in the nineties.

That was actually the last of the high adventures at 111 Main Street. Now that I was only washing dishes on Saturdays, I spent more time sitting before the bureau in my back room above the kitchen, trying to restore my damaged grades. The fact that I had only a few weeks of high school left, instead of the whole year I'd anticipated, gave a real urgency to my homework. The prospect of college was looming even nearer than I imagined. But which? My father had gone to prep school and to Princeton. Back in the days before World War I, and before Prohibition had ruined the family finances, a couple of my great-uncles had gone to Lehigh on Lehigh Valley Railroad scholarships. Our stepfather had gone to Hobart College in Geneva, New York, and then to the Harvard Business School. When he and I discussed colleges, he said it seemed to him that anyone in his right mind who had a chance of going to Harvard had to take it. I said I would send for an application.

No one believes this now, but on the day I decided to write to

Harvard, I realized I hadn't the faintest idea where Harvard was, except that it was in the East. I looked in the *World Almanac* and discovered that it was in Cambridge, Massachusetts, and that its address bore the postal zone number (a primitive, two-digit zip code) 38. I received a terse letter from the Admissions Office, saying it was rather late to be applying but that I was welcome to send a transcript, and I had better arrange to take the College Board exams, which were being given at Syracuse University the following weekend. Life is full of misses and near misses. If I'd waited another week to write my letter of application, I might well have missed the college boards, with possibly dire consequences.

The application also required the transcript of all my high school grades to date, including midterm grades for the current semester. One day, I was stopped after class by Clarissa P. Heaton, my wonderfully eccentric history teacher. I can still hear Mrs. Heaton's perky voice, as I can Mrs. Labby's. "Charles," she said sternly, "when you began, you were doing A work. Then you went to that dreadful restaurant to wash dishes and your work went to blazes. You didn't do your homework and frankly you were doing C work." Then she paused and gave a conspiratorial grin. "But I remember some very wise remarks in class and the good work at the beginning." She paused again. "And, besides, no one from this school has gone to Harvard in fifty years. So I'm putting you in for an A." I remain convinced that it was Clarissa P. Heaton who got me into Harvard singlehandedly and, along with Don Barker, helped change my life.

I actually took the College Boards that Saturday in Syracuse. Pop drove me in to the University. My only distinct memory of the event is sitting on stone steps, enjoying the thin, late winter sunlight before we went inside, and feeling unusually calm. It was too late to worry, I told myself. I had no real conviction that Harvard would take me, ergo, I had nothing to lose—which was far from the truth.

Back in Camden, I worked hard for the final Regents Exams. I

CAMDEN HIGH SCHOOL GRADUATION PHOTO: *I see myself at seventeen looking astonishingly young, immature, and unready for the real world, but bearing a look of quiet determination.*

suppose my last vivid memory of the Camden school days was the night of the Senior Prom when, toward midnight, three of us couples strode down Second Street, six abreast, singing "For Me and My Gal" at the top of our voices with some sense that the great world beckoned and we were ready for it. I had, it turned out, restored my grades sufficiently so that I ended up second in the class, behind a lovely young woman who became a teacher.

While I was studying for the Regents, a letter came from Cambridge 38, saying I'd been accepted for the Class of 1947, and adding that the College was now operating year-round and I was due in Harvard Square at the beginning of July. I couldn't quite believe the news. But, perhaps without being aware of it, I'd always thought that destiny was on my side because I realized I hadn't bothered to apply anywhere else. I've wondered, across this half century, whether there was any other moment in history when I could have gotten into Harvard College. We were at war; there may have been a shortage of applicants (although 1,100 of us showed up). It all worked out fine in the end, but I did think Harvard had made a mistake.

Harvard

E ven now I see myself on a steamy, early July day in 1943, lugging a cheap, heavy, black, fake leather suitcase through South Station in Boston, in quest of the subway to Harvard Square. There could be no doubt that I was arriving at a wartime Harvard. There were men in a variety of uniforms rushing in every direction, and here and there I could see couples standing close to each other but saying little in those terrible last moments when there is nothing else to say but good-bye. I'm afraid I looked exactly as I was, a freshman arriving in Boston in all the wrong clothes. I was wearing a canvas hat because my stepfather had said that everybody in Cambridge wore hats, which might have been true when he was there in the late 1920s. I was also wearing a shirt and tie and a double-breasted, chocolate brown pinstriped suit that I'd bought by mail order from Montgomery Ward. How I came to buy that particular suit is still a mystery to me. It might have had to do with some misplaced film fantasy. George Raft would have looked great in it. I felt ridiculous and I'm sure I looked ridiculous. I think I only wore it one more time when I posed for a formal portrait to give Mother for Christmas.

I lugged my suitcase up the stairs from the Harvard Square tube station and into the Square itself. Here in all its splendid image was Harvard, the brick dormitories along Massachusetts Avenue, the street crowds well populated by young Harvard men. I asked my

44

way to Lowell House, one of the elegant dormitories in the tradition of the Oxford and Cambridge houses. In peacetime, Lowell and the other houses were reserved for upperclassmen. In wartime, the dormitories in the Harvard Yard were full of servicemen, as they'd been two hundred years before when George Washington's troops occupied them. I stopped at the small office at the entrance to Lowell and was directed to K-42, an apartment on the fourth floor of K entry. I knocked tentatively. And so began another chapter of my life.

There were four of us in an apartment intended for two, with two double bunks. I soon saw how shrewdly the housing officials had assigned us, especially considering how little time they'd had to cope with so many of us.

All four of us were Roman Catholics, although a couple of us may have strayed slightly. We were all from the East but not of the New England elite from the more elegant prep schools (which their grandfathers may well have attended). The preppies tended to gravitate naturally to the power positions in the class and publications.

John Adikes, Jr., the son of a savings banker in Jamaica, Long Island, had attended Xavier, a military high school in Manhattan run by the Jesuits. He was sturdy, handsome, with a crew cut (brush cut is probably more accurate), decisive, outspoken, incredibly smart and, at seventeen, already had a commanding presence—although, as events were soon to prove, Jack also had a mischievous streak that was equally commanding. A half century later, I discovered, when the director John Frankenheimer (*The Manchurian Candidate*) and I were doing a long series of interviews, that he was a close cousin of Jack's. Jack was a few years older, and John, who'd attended a different military high school, had regarded Jack as a combination of idol and mentor.

Robert J. Carey was out of the excellent Newton High School at the west edge of Boston. His family ran a furniture store. He was a passionate admirer of Winston Churchill and could recite long passages from his speeches, including Churchill's unforgettable address to Parliament after the debacle of Dunkirk in 1939. I can still quote some of its concluding oratory, commencing with, "We shall fight on the beaches, we shall fight on the landing grounds," and so on, and rising to "And if, which I do not for a moment believe, this Island or a large part of it were subjugated and starving, then our Empire beyond the seas, armed and guarded by the British fleet, would carry on the struggle, until, in God's good time, the New World, with all its power and might, steps forth to the rescue and liberation of the Old." It thrills me still. At frequent intervals, Bob also burst into the song of the British Grenadiers ("Some speak of Alexander, and some of Hercules . . .").

When Bob and I met again in Los Angeles a half century later, he confessed that, despite his outward breezy confidence, he felt he lacked a sense of direction and envied what he thought was Jack's and my purposefulness. That August, Bob rushed off to enlist in the Marines, the first of the foursome to leave. He hoped to find his purpose and try Harvard again after the war, as he did, most successfully.

Russell Whitney Gross was another Long Islander, as passionate about classical music as Bob was about Churchill, and devoted to the insightful if often irascible reviews of B. H. Haggin in the *Nation*. Russ had the habit (unique in my experience) of staring, as if for guidance, at the nail on his left little finger, when he was saying something of particular moment, humorous or otherwise. I think he was the most devout among us, Jack a close second, and Bob and I also-rans. Russ became at least briefly a follower of Father Leonard Feeney, who preached for a while at the nearby St. Paul the Apostle Church, until he was silenced by the Cardinal for insisting that there was no salvation outside the Catholic Church. Then, as always in his life, Russ liked things black or white, not gray.

Years later, after Russ's marriage broke up, he found his way to a fundamentalist Christian commune in Maine. He lived by its strict

disciplines, played competitive tennis into his sixties, made his living selling insurance and found great serenity in the rigors of his
faith. He died in an automobile accident only a few days before our
50th reunion. He wouldn't have come anyway, having severed his
emotional ties with the College over what, in his now conservative
views, he regarded as its permissiveness in all things.

It was a curious time we four shared. The war was in its second
year for America, in its fifth for Europe—longer if you count Mus-
solini's invasion of Ethiopia, and still longer in Asia, where Japan
had been battling China since the four of us were just out of kinder-
garten. War was part of our daily lives in Cambridge. Soldiers and
sailors marched to class, singing in cadence. Uniforms were more
frequent than tweed jackets in the Yard.

But in that summer and fall of 1943, we in the Class of 1947 were
a kind of civilian island amid the sea of war news. Even though it
was July not September when we entered, and we were living in the
upperclassmen's housing, we were Harvard freshman, the three
hundred and seventh such gathering. Like several dozen freshman
assemblies before us, we schemed to avoid eight o'clock classes if we
could. That year we tried to avoid one o'clock classes as well, rather
than miss a local team of radio comics named Bob and Ray.

The foolishnesses of Bob and Ray were a respite from the war
news we obviously couldn't ignore. The invasion of Italy was not far
off; the Germans were in trouble in Russia. Every day, if it did not
bring the war closer to us, brought us closer to the war. The edgy
question was how we would sooner or later fit into the picture.

For the moment, we all tried to make the most of our time and
savor the Harvard experience, different as it now was. Even in its
wartime guise, which somehow gave it a more populist atmosphere
(the presence of the servicemen, and the wives of the Navy officers),
I was awed by the College's reputation, and its antiquity. There
seemed to be three centuries' worth of ghosts hanging about, from

Cotton Mather in precolonial days to William Randolph Hearst, who'd been tossed out for some anti-faculty pranks. The names of Harvard's Civil War dead were incised in white marble on the walls of Memorial Hall. The uphill walk from Lowell to the Yard went past the Lampoon Building, the Crimson and the Hasty Pudding Club, and I never quite got over the excitement of the scenery, fascinating but remote from me because, as a rural outlander, I could never imagine being part of those establishment scenes. They were not likely to be part of my Harvard, then or ever or, rather, I would never be part of those places.

On almost my first day in Cambridge, I'd stumbled onto a used copy of George Weller's fine 1933 novel about Harvard, *Not to Eat, Not for Love* (a quote from Emerson). I identified strongly with one of his characters who was himself an outsider, working his way through Harvard delivering the *Crimson* early in the morning. The novel, like my solitary walks up to the Yard and through it, defined who I was, and who I was not—I was not yet a Harvard man.

We used to go across the street to a deli that we discovered made ultra-thick frappes and peanut butter sandwiches of such incredibly gummy goodness that they stuck to the roof of your mouth and had to be dislodged by the tongue. We brought back the sandwiches and the frappes (in glass milk bottles) for late night snacks in K-42. The bottles were the inspiration for Jack's sturdy but occasionally juvenile sense of fun. He proposed—and the others of us went along with a kind of dread anticipation—that we fill the bottles with water, put them in their paper bags and drop them down the stairwell to the stone floor at the bottom. They hit with bomb-like booms, which raised angry shouts from the lower floors, plus a visit from security and a summons to the Master's office.

The Master of Lowell House was then Elliott Perkins, a tall, lean, bald historian already famous for his bulletin board memos, couched in a style I have characterized as a blend of the *New Yorker* and *The Book of Common Prayer.* Mr. Perkins was not amused by the bottle bombing, but he seemed to have understood, accurately enough, that we were freshmen and not long for his world. Jack quickly admitted his authorship of the idea, and we were all let off with a reprimand.

In every way Harvard in mid-war was a truly remarkable place, not least for someone from a village in upstate New York. The refugee Italian anti-Fascist scholar Gaetano Salvemini lived in Lowell House and was daily to be seen walking to the dining hall, hands clasped behind him European-style and lost in thoughts I could not begin to imagine. Heinrich Brüning, who'd been chancellor of Germany until forced out by the Nazis in 1934, had been at Harvard since 1936. He, too, lived in Lowell, a somber-looking man who seemed preoccupied with his contemplations of an appalling time.

One of the features confronting Harvard freshmen was, and perhaps still is, the "English A Anticipatory Exam," a written test of thought and fluency, which separates those who have to take the mandatory freshman English course from those who are excused from it. I flunked the exam, and so did Russ and Bob. Jack, who I don't believe had any aspirations to write, breezed through it, a tribute to his Jesuit education. I brooded about this for days. My ambition for as long as I could remember had been to make my way as a writer, but to fail the Anticipatory Exam felt like a dreadful omen. I saw that my contemporaries, like Jack, who'd attended demanding prep schools, had been pushed and encouraged to high standards of analysis and interpretation. I realized even before I attended my first class that I had some catching up to do.

One of the section men teaching English A that year was Wallace Stegner, whose novel *The Big Rock Candy Mountain* had only recently been published, to great acclaim. I wanted very much to study with him, but so did everybody else, and his section was oversubscribed. When I moved to Los Angeles in 1959, I began to read his nonfiction books about the West, as well as his fine later novels. Stegner was, I thought then and feel now, the shrewdest interpreter of the real West we had, loving it but sharply critical of the overexploitation of an essentially arid land. I met him at last in the early 1990s, and I had a chance to tell him how I admired his work, and how I regretted not taking English A from him. He remembered his days at Harvard fondly, but he'd been glad, I think, to move back West. We corresponded occasionally until his tragic death in 1993, when he was struck by a car on a visit to Albuquerque.

The textbook devised by Harvard's English Department and entitled *Five Kinds of Writing* is still on my shelf, a provocative anthology quite aside from its classroom function, and the more entertaining to browse in today, when there is no threat of quizzes. My instructor, who seemed to me then to be a senior faculty member, was probably a Ph.D. candidate working his way along. Each week, we were instructed to write themes of one thousand words or so on any subject we chose. The sheer volume of writing demanded, probably as much as anything else, went a long way toward making a real writer out of me, but the discipline required was also far different from anything I'd experienced before. My wonderful high school teachers, Miss Dorothy Becker in my junior year and Miss Doris McGee in my senior year, had understood that I had an urge to write that not everyone did, and they encouraged me to write whatever I wanted. They said, "Go, go, go," and I went, writing purely by instinct, with little sense of formal structure.

English A at Harvard was a great leap into a new dimension. My instructor was rigorous in his comments on the themes we wrote. I learned to develop goals in my writing, to focus on the direction of an essay so that you know where you're going and how to get there. My grades rose slowly, as in the ascent of a difficult mountain, and I realized that my mornings in Warren House, the ancient wooden building where the English Department was headquartered, were invaluable.

Occasionally I would sneak a glance at the graded essays awaiting collection by their authors from mail slots in the office. The intellectual density of some of them was formidable, and the fictions were darkly tragic. I did not yet have anything like a literary voice I could call my own. That voice finally arises unbidden, as I once noted, out of everything you have seen, felt and read and liked, and out of the process of writing itself. I got a glimmering of this truth during my days in English A. I began to think that I was on the right track, if a long way from wherever I was going, and it was a relieving if teasing thought.

The infamous midterm hour exams were my first traumatic confrontations with Harvard standards. They were the more ominous for being printed, not mimeographed or scrawled on blackboards. I have preserved a few of those hour exam question sheets somewhere, and when I read them now I still can't imagine how I was able to answer them at all. The worst were the essay questions (which seemed only distantly related to whatever you'd read or heard in lectures). They made a statement and then simply said, "Discuss." O terrifying word, "Discuss." Nothing so simple as tossing in a few facts retained from all-night cramming. It was meaning that was sought—which was, as I'd already begun to appreciate, the way it should be. But it was a strained step up from the exams I'd known before, when memory, regurgitated, would get you around almost any corner.

One of the prewar maxims at Harvard was said to have been "Three C's and a D and keep your name out of the papers." This may have been so in those legendary years between the great wars, but it seemed absurdly irrelevant in 1943. You might have thought that our foreshortened taste of college would be observed as a last fling—a time to eat, drink, and be merry while you still could. I think it was true that we all grabbed as many of the pleasures of Cambridge and Boston as we could afford. Money was a big factor in the way the four of us conducted our lives, and while Jack was, I suppose, the best fixed of us all, he was prudent, to say the least.

Yet the predominating impulse among us was to make the most of college. We all studied like hell. Lacking a typewriter, I scrawled themes into the wee hours, occasionally on my lap in the bathroom when the others were sleeping.

Jack and I joined the ROTC and were issued uniforms with identifying blue lapels. There were at most not quite twenty of us in the unit. But, under the command of our leader, Captain Nelson P. Hoadley, a peacetime insurance agent from Connecticut, we practiced close-order drill beside the Charles, feeling as foolish as we looked and meeting once a week for classes in military science and tactics. Jack, who probably knew more of these matters than the captain did, was our unofficial leader. Why Jack bothered with ROTC, I don't know. The rest of us had an idea (ludicrous as it turned out) that the experience would give us a head start when we actually went in service.

Jack, ever the urger, one night proposed that he and I go to a dance hall in our uniforms and meet some girls. I've forgotten the name of the place, but it was large and popular and distinctly town, not gown. I tended to be shy, not to say timid, and I had visions of us getting nailed as Harvard snobs masquerading as GIs. If asked, we agreed to say we were a special unit, which was true as far as it went, which wasn't far. Jack carried it off beautifully, and we even danced with some very nice girls. But I found the role was too hard to sustain and we only ventured out that once.

I'd always liked jazz, loved it actually, but I'd never had many chances to hear it live. One day, the *Harvard Service News* (the wartime version of the *Crimson*) reported that Duke Ellington was going to speak on the history of jazz in New Lecture Hall that afternoon. I got there early. I really knew jazz only from the radio, especially the remotes from hotels and nightclubs across the country, but Ellington was already one of my heroes. Even then, I realized that his appearance was a publicity stunt. The band was playing at a theater in Boston and his appearance at Harvard was what a later time would call a "photo op." The Duke entered to great applause, seated himself at a grand piano, declared that he loved us all madly, and began to play a medley of his songs, "Sophisticated Lady," "Take the A Train," and others, interspersing brief remarks about New Orleans, Chicago, and the Cotton Club. A photographer from the theater pulled five of us from the audience, including a couple of ensigns, and posed us around the piano, grinning reverentially. After I went in service, I asked Mother to write the theater to see if it could supply a print of one of the Ellington event pictures. They were kind enough to send one, and I prize it above all my mementos of the time. By one of those happy swings of fate, Reprise Records asked me in the 1970s to write some liner notes for a new Ellington album. A few months later, the band was performing at Disneyland and I met the Duke again, introduced by his friend, Leonard Feather, the jazz critic of the *Los Angeles Times,* who'd written the first jazz waltz Ellington ever recorded. The Duke autographed my album, and said he loved me madly.

One of the GIs taking courses that summer was Staff Sergeant George Avakian, in peacetime a record producer for the Columbia label. Some of his musician pals were appearing at the Brauhaus in nearby Lawrence, Massachusetts, and George arranged for them to come and play on two Saturday afternoons in the Lowell House dining hall. I forget what the admission was but I'd have spent every cent I had and borrowed more to be there.

I didn't know enough then to realize quite what a piece of jazz history I was hearing. Art Hodes was there, making an upright piano rock with the power of his striding left hand. Another near-legendary figure, Mezz Mezzrow, was on clarinet and still another, Frankie Newton, played trumpet. Mezzrow's book, *Really the Blues,* was an early confessional account of the jazz life, and marijuana's role in it. The drummer was Kaiser Marshall, a storied player him-

DUKE ELLINGTON AT HARVARD: *The Duke at Harvard in early 1944 talked about jazz, mostly his own, before an enraptured audience that included Charles Champlin, about to enter the Army. The Navy officers were training at the College. From left: William Nyhan, Duke Ellington, Rockwell Colaneri, unidentified ensigns, Charles Champlin.*

self, and I think Miff Mole was on trombone, although I can't recall the name of the bassist.

I'd never before heard live, improvised jazz, with its extended solos and with their "All hands on deck" ride-out choruses. On one of the afternoons, the band marched out of the hall playing "The Saints Go Marching In." It was supremely corny, as we all realized, but it was wonderful just the same. And the concerts wedded me forever to improvised rather than written-down jazz and to the imaginative and virtuoso skills of great instrumentalists.

One night, I went to the Boston Garden, where the great vibes player Lionel Hampton was appearing with his orchestra. He featured two double basses, the king-size versions that rested on stands. Hampton's best-known recording was "Flying Home" and he concluded the concert with it. It went on for chorus after chorus, led by Hampton himself, with extended solos by his great sidemen. All the while, the double basses set up a pulsing beat of such intensity that you didn't so much hear it as feel it. It seemed to vibrate even through the balcony where I was sitting. It was one of the most extraordinary evenings of big band jazz that I'd ever heard and that still surpasses in memory anything I have heard since.

The war years and the postwar classes speeded up the geographic democratization of Harvard that had been under way in the early 1940s. From the beginning, Harvard had, of course, been a New England institution and well into the 1930s the greater proportion of those who came to Harvard did not have far to go from home. In the college annuals, addresses in Massachusetts, Maine, New Hampshire, Vermont, and New York City predominated. I found later that Harvard had been making considerable efforts to broaden its base, encouraging students from all over the country and, indeed, from many countries overseas. I couldn't make comparisons between the Harvard of 1943 and those of previous years, but it was obvious, in 1943, that many of us had our beginnings far from the New England elite. I think that most of the classmates I came to know were, like the four of us, what you might call "Harvard irregulars."

I suppose that, if you've attended Harvard, ever after you are a Harvard man. I never really knew what a Harvard man was. Remembering my canvas hat and the double-breasted brown suit, I was sure that I wasn't a Harvard man. It was not until my twenty-fifth reunion that I began to think, by damn, I *am* a Harvard man. By then, I'd gotten some attention as a film critic (quoted occasionally in ads in the *New York Times,* probably when I was taking a positive but minority view of a film). This wasn't, I don't think, a form of bragging; just a recognition that I'd achieved some minor triumph. One of my classmates, Cliff Wharton, had become the first African American to be president of Michigan State. The joke is that at the twenty-fifth reunion, everybody brags about how well he's doing. At the fortieth, everyone brags about having retired and become a consultant. At the fiftieth, everyone is simply pleased to be around. My own feeling, from the twenty-fifth onward, was that simple survival is a highly efficient leveler. Whatever distinctions you had recognized or felt during college days had somehow faded away.

In early October, I was handed a telegram. It was from Pop and said, in toto, "A daughter has arrived." Pop was a man of considerable thriftiness, but he could have used six more words for the same price. He neglected to give his new daughter's name or any report on how Mother was doing. She was having a baby at forty-five, thirteen years since Joe was born, and it had been worrying and suspenseful for all of us. But when I called home, I learned that the baby's name was Nancy and that Mother and she were doing fine. The new baby, an astonishment not least to her parents when they learned she was on the way, was a wonderful affirmation of the marriage and of Mother's new life. As it happened, I felt other emotions that Saturday morning when the telegram arrived. I would thereafter be only a temporary visitor to Cleveland and only an occasional witness to Nancy's growing up and to the new family that Pop and Mother were building. Although that was the way my life went, I've always regretted not having been a closer part of those experiences.

What you experience outside the classroom is of course as much a part of an education as what you learn inside. For my part, I saw my first live dramas at the Brattle Theater in Cambridge, including a production of Eugene O'Neill's *Emperor Jones*. One of the greater glories was the chance to see foreign films. The only films that had been screened in Hammondsport were by Frank Buck and featured large snakes and great cats. And while I am not certain exactly when I saw them—in my first year at Harvard or when I returned after the war—films like *Open City* and *Les Enfants du Paradis* made indelible marks on my psyche and propelled me toward film criticism when that option arose in my life.

Early in our second term, with Bob Carey off to the Marines, Jack and Russ and I and some of our other friends went off to the recruiting center on Commonwealth Avenue in downtown Boston and joined the Army's Enlisted Reserve Corps (ERC). What this meant was that you were an enlistee, not a draftee, with a "1" instead of a "3" in front of your serial number. Jack's was 11-133-422; mine was 11-133-489. Being an enlistee gave us a spurious sense that we were in charge of our own destinies, for the moment at least, and were patriots as well. More practically, joining the ERC also allowed us to volunteer for induction at an appropriate point in our college work (not long after we turned eighteen, of course, but at least we weren't at the mercy of a draft board).

Jack left in early February 1944, just ahead of the second term finals, as I recall, and went off to take paratrooper training at Camp Blanding, Florida. He bequeathed me some of his elegant Brooks Brothers neckties and I wore them for years, until they wore out.

The breakup of the bottle droppers meant that Russ and I had to be reassigned to new rooms. Russ briefly joined some other friends and I went to F-42 to room with Robin Worthington, a tall and charming Southerner from Jacksonville, Florida. Robin had left for the Army with great flourishes, but was back a few days later, having been found to have a dysfunctional knee, and looking slightly sheepish. (Ironically, he was called into service after all, but at the time of the Korean War, when he was already practicing law.)

After more than fifty years, the times of these events have long since blurred, but Russ I think went on active duty not long after Jack. As the youngest of the four of us, I had a few more weeks in Cambridge. But in March I turned eighteen and I volunteered for induction in May, midway through the first term of my sophomore year. I hadn't been resident in Cambridge a year, only ten months in fact, and here I was a sophomore. This was, then and in years to come, a disappointment. I'd had a Harvard education as far as I'd gone, and its effects had already changed my life and expanded my mind, inducing a new way of seeing and thinking. Yet I couldn't feel that I'd had the whole Harvard experience.

As I repacked the old steamer trunk Mother had used when she went to Vassar in 1918, I hoped I'd get back to Harvard one day. I suppose I should say I hoped I'd survive the war, period. As the basic infantry rifleman I would surely become, survival was not assured. But Harvard had already changed my life and enlarged my vision of the world. I wanted more of the Harvard experience, especially the peacetime Harvard that George Weller had described.

Russ Gross and I stayed in touch for years; we met frequently when we were both working in New York, Russ building a career in the insurance business, I as a trainee then a junior writer at *Life*. We met once more at the twenty-fifth reunion; thereafter, we exchanged letters until the last years of his life. Often in those last years, he would send me religious tracts, sometimes with handwritten exhortations in the margins for me to read and think about.

Bob Carey I did not see for many years. He had become a teacher, mostly in Connecticut while I was a continent away in California. Bob's daughter is a brilliant dramatist working with the Cornerstone Theater in Los Angeles; Bob and I last got together when he came out West to see her.

Jack Adikes went to Officer Candidate School at Fort Benning, Georgia, became an infantry second lieutenant, and died in action in Luxembourg. The life expectancy of infantry lieutenants was short indeed, as Jack himself proved.

So the foursome that met in July 1943 has become a twosome— with only Bob Carey and me still alive as I write.

The Army

From at least sixth grade forward, war was a large part of my consciousness. The Spanish Civil War was ripping that lovely country apart when I was twelve, although it was a long time before I understood all the politics of it: the Loyalists versus Francisco Franco and the Rebels. The newspapers carried many stories and photographs, but none more indelibly affecting than *Life*'s photograph of a Spanish soldier leaping into a trench at the exact instant a bullet emerges from his skull.

I must have been particularly sensitive to the idea of war. Certainly from sixth and seventh grades onward, when I was eleven and twelve, war seemed like a gray cloud on the distant horizon, but coming closer to the United States and right along toward me.

The European war had broken out in August 1939, and the papers now were full of photographs of the skies filled with German fighters and bombers, German tanks rolling through the Low Countries, and the roads lined with refugees.

Despite the forebodings, the Japanese attack on Pearl Harbor caught us all by surprise, as it did the American armed forces in the Pacific. On that Sunday afternoon in upstate New York, six of us had loaded into Howard Curtiss's Essex and driven south to Bath for an afternoon of bowling. We heard about the attack as we left the bowling alley. Not one of us in the Essex could have told you within two thousand miles where Pearl Harbor was. I remember one of the group, Bill Brady I think it was, saying something like "Those stupid yellow jerks, we'll take care of them in six weeks." But it was going to be far longer than six weeks before we'd have the war behind us and be together again.

The fighting was two oceans away, but the war was nevertheless upon us. Gasoline was beginning to be rationed; rubber goods like hot water bottles were in short supply; there were battle stars in many of the windows; and many of the older guys were coming home on furloughs, tanned and healthy from the rigorous basic training, mostly done in the Southern states where the big infantry training camps were. Most of them would be reporting to other camps, where divisions were being formed and trained, before they shipped out for overseas battle assignment.

The fighting was far off; we read about it in the Rochester or Syracuse newspapers or listened to it on the radio, as we did to the steadying voice of Elmer Davis each night just before nine. Radio was in fact central to my life in those pretelevision days. There were the often staticky broadcasts from overseas, with Edward R. Murrow on a London rooftop, unforgettably describing a night of bombing during the Battle of Britain.

For me, at fifteen going on sixteen, it was a kind of split-level life. There were the high school goings-on, sock hops, and basketball games and the usual sweating before exams or laboring over homework. But, against all those aspects of "normalcy," there was this new awareness that nothing was going to be exactly the same again.

Now, at seventeen, I'd enlisted and, just after my eighteenth birthday, in 1944, I went on active duty.

In an ironic way, starting my life in the Army was like Harvard all over again. I felt out of my depth—I never imagined, even as the prospect drew nearer, that I would make much of a warrior. As a bookish, introspective, and fairly unassertive teenager, I didn't see myself as a leader of men, certainly not at just barely eighteen, and looking even younger than that. (I kept being asked for my ID until I was well into my twenties.) And then, too, I wore glasses and couldn't do without them. None of the GIs you saw in the war movies wore glasses, except maybe the squad goof-up who, if he was lucky, accidentally did something brave and helpful and died and was mourned by the guys who'd made fun of him before. A great role.

So I went off to service with even less confidence than I'd had when I hit Cambridge. But I desperately wanted to succeed at Harvard and I desperately wanted to succeed in the Army, to restore my self-esteem for a start. Beyond that, I believed fervently in the war— we all did—and I wanted to help.

Like the Harvard beginnings in another way, my months in the Army now present themselves as occasional detailed scenes rather than as a continuous narrative. Between the memorable moments, I remember little of my day-to-day life. I have no recollection at all of taking the train from Oneida (probably) or Rome (possibly) to Grand Central Station, or how I knew I was to report to Penn Station, or how I got there.

My first recollection of that May 22nd, 1944, is of a near-disaster that did my self-esteem no good at all. The sergeant who met us at the station—there were five of us inductees bound for Fort Dix—entrusted me to carry the paperwork for the whole group. As we rattled along to Wrightstown, the stop for Fort Dix, I was lost in fantasies about the immediate future, or perhaps in dramatic melancholy over Fern, the girl I was leaving behind. Wherever I was in my head, when we got off at Wrightstown, I left our precious papers behind. I came to my senses in the nick of time and rushed back aboard and retrieved the documents before the train pulled out and went on to Philadelphia. My fellow passengers regarded me with well-deserved scorn, but said nothing. They were probably distracted by imaginings of their own. Mine now included a narrow escape from beginning my Army career with punishment for being a nerdy incompetent.

The sequence of events at an induction center had already been so well exposed in newsreels and movies—Abbott and Costello in *Buck Privates* was an early version—that I had the feeling I'd been there before. There were the long lines, as at a cafeteria, during which your Army uniform, from cap to boots, was thrust onto your arms until the tottering pile was high as your head, just the way it was in the funny movies. Changing into your uniform (olive drab fatigues, actually) was a perfect metaphor for shedding your civilian self, including not least your individuality and your command of your own destiny.

The worst of those feelings lay ahead, as when, in basic training, you encountered the corporals and sergeants who seemed to take a sadistic delight in demonstrating how anonymous and how powerless you were. The passes to town cancelled arbitrarily, the midnight scrubbings of a barracks as punishment for some infraction of previously undisclosed rules, the extra push-ups to atone for calisthenics alleged to be slackly done—all imposed in the name of making us unquestioningly obedient soldiers.

No one would have mistaken me for an athlete, even in poor light. But I was glad to be in the Army. I didn't have to see Frank Capra's highly effective *Why We Fight* training films (although I did) to understand what the war was about, and why it had to be won, and how it was that even I had a part to play. More than half a century later, our certainty about our war, the lack of any ambiguity about why we were in the fight we were in, looks like a curious luxury denied to those who'd volunteered or been conscripted to fight in Vietnam and, almost as cloudily, in Korea before that. Looking back, I don't think I was wrong about the need to fight. At the time, I see a naïve and sentimental fellow too willing to ignore the slings and arrows of unpleasant noncoms in basic training in the name of "The Cause."

But in that warm early summer of 1944, I was off to war. From the start, I had three deeply felt but unexpressed fears. One of them, obviously, was that I would be killed in action. I told myself that it was likely to be quick and probably painless. One of the bits of lore that circulated in training camp was that you never hear the shot that gets you. I found out later that this was often true. My really terrifying fear was that I might survive, but come home maimed or blinded and helpless. The third fear was that I might die before I married and had children, might indeed die a virgin (having, through no lack of trying, remained technically chaste). As I wrote in *Back There Where the Past Was*, the idea of continuing the family line was uncommonly strong in someone as young as I was. My family had been in the same village for a hundred years. Our line ran from an ancestor captured by the Indians before the American Revolution, to my father who died when I was twelve, and finally to me. My younger brother was clearly destined for the priesthood. Thus it fell to me to continue the family line. Otherwise, our branch of the family tree would end with me. From Fort Dix, hundreds of us boarded the train for Camp Croft in the red clay of South Carolina. By now, all the train rides from my Army days have merged into one long, endless journey. It was always oppressively hot and gritty in the ancient cars, innocent of air conditioning, and always crowded to the point of standing room only. What air there was was always blue with cigarette smoke, to which I contributed in those days. The trip south to Spartanburg, the nearest city to Camp Croft, established the pattern and only the scenery changed.

It was probably impossible to tell one of those huge infantry training camps from another. They came from the same sets of plans and were assembly-line designed to turn out soldiers in seventeen hard weeks. Nor, I suspect, did the graffiti in the latrines vary much from camp to camp. My favorite was "Please do not throw cigarette butts in the urinals. It makes them soggy and hard to light. Signed,

The Captain." Another, also in the latrines, was "Bulls with short horns stand close."

Our barracks was divided almost equally between those of us from the Northeast—New York and New Jersey mostly—and draftees from Tennessee and the Carolinas. These were young men from the hills and hollows of Appalachia, with strong accents that hinted not so much of the South as of distant origins in the British Isles. Most of them were bunked on the second floor of the barracks, and in the evenings before taps they used to sing hymns in the wonderful close harmony I associate with bluegrass music. There were anthems I'd never heard. "There was dust on the Bible, dust on the Holy Word" went one and "I heard the wreck on the highway, but I didn't hear nobody pray" went another. As good old boys will, they kept to themselves, banding together against those of us who talked mighty Yankee and were from Northern cities whose images were violent and foreign in the extreme. Our numbers included some Jews, and I suspect many of the hill men had never seen a Jew before. In their way, the Appalachians probably felt as displaced as we did. We drilled and marched and sweated together, but socially the men on the second floor kept well clear of us.

By now, not only were the services grabbing all of us young men as we turned eighteen, but they'd also begun calling up previously deferred married men with children. One of the men in our barracks had been a car dealer in Albany, I think. He was overweight and out of shape. I worried that Earl would not survive basic, but somehow he did, groaning all the way. There was a music teacher from some other town upstate who played marvelous cornet and still another fellow who'd been a farmer in a place called Stone Arabia, which I have never been able to locate on a New York state map. I have a feeling the town was so small it finally vanished altogether.

Filling out the endless forms at Fort Dix, I'd indicated that I played the cornet. I never thought anybody would find this of interest for a minute, but the Army is full of surprises. It turned out that many of us on the main floor of the barracks, like the teacher from upstate, were in what was called "Buglers School." We did all the usual things everyone else did in basic training—the close-order drill (aimed at crushing out any faint, lingering traces of individuality); the 25-mile hikes; the firing range after we learned to field strip and reassemble our M-l rifles again and again; the dreaded infiltration course where you crawled under barbed wire while live ammo crackled overhead, your mind filled with old sergeants' tales of copperheads and other poisonous snakes slithering onto the course; the hygiene lectures (one corporal used to drone on about "va-rious mala-rious a-reas")—all that and the barracks scrubbings and other instructive punishments.

But occasionally, of an afternoon, we buglers would be led off into the woods, where we'd sit around and practice bugle calls. Buglers were understood to be messengers when they weren't bugling, so we also had sessions with a portable encoding machine that looked very much like an adding machine. I never saw one again and never got to blow a bugle in or out of combat.

I had fifteen minutes or so of celebrity when a high school girl friend (platonic) sent me a copy of Walter Benton's slim, lavender-jacketed book of poems, *This Is My Beloved,* which even then had sold hundreds of thousands of copies and can still be found in bookstores. The poems, on the flowering and the wilting of a romance in the shadow of the war, were highly erotic by the standards of the time, and the enveloping theme of love lost had a special appeal to men even temporarily without women. Every man on our floor read the book the night I received it, and an unaccustomed silence fell over the barracks, as the readers retired to their own long thoughts.

I've probably never been in better physical shape than I was when I went home on furlough after my seventeen weeks of basic training. Having gained fifteen hard pounds, I went out on the front lawn to fall face forward on my hands to show off my new strength and agility. Mother was suitably impressed, although her worst fears about my going into combat peeked through her cheerful bravery.

The transit papers I was handed as I left Camp Croft, mimeographed on cheap paper and written in that cryptic military prose that always favors the passive voice ("It is ordered . . ."), granted me a 14-day furlough and then ordered me to report to Fort Leonard Wood, Missouri, there to join the 70th Division. But the division I was joining had no need of a bugler—or even of another body. It shipped out without me. I went next to Fort Meade, Maryland, where I did a certain amount of KP and stood guard with a wooden rifle over the post laundry, where the cheerful black women sang along with a portable radio. Their favorite song was "My Dreams Are Getting Better All the Time." I hear it rarely anymore, but when I do I am back in the warm night air of Maryland.

After a short stay at Meade, I was sent on to Camp Miles Standish, near Taunton, Massachusetts, an embarkation camp for troops sailing out of Boston. Where we were was ostensibly a close-kept military secret. The posters warned that "Loose Talk Costs Lives," and I believed it wholeheartedly and somehow imagined Axis agents behind each tree and tapping every phone call. I wangled a pass into Boston, took the subway out to Harvard, and walked down to Lowell House, where a few of my pals were still around. Calling Mother from the pay phone in the dining room, I told her that I was at the dorm, but (in case the enemy was listening) I didn't mention Harvard, Lowell House, Cambridge, or even Boston, let alone Miles Standish. The Army would have been terribly proud of me, but the effect was a bit compromised by the chaplain at Miles Standish, Reverend Guy Madeira, who'd been the Episcopal priest in Hammondsport. He saw my name on a roster and called Mother to say I was in good hands, so I hadn't surprised her at all.

When I went back into Boston to catch a train to the camp, the cab

drivers were all saying, "Need a ride to Standish?" as if I were holding a cardboard sign. So much for secrecy. I took a cab.

By now, it was the end of November and the weather was bitter
cold and windy. We had a splendid turkey dinner for Thanksgiving—the last such feast for many a day. Then we embarked. Our ship
out of Boston was a peacetime liner named the USS *Manhattan*, although it may have had a different civilian name. The weather was
vile as we sailed out of the harbor. The *Manhattan* was old and not
large, and it clearly lacked the stabilizers now standard on modern
cruise ships. We bucked fore and aft and lurched drunkenly from
side to side. It was a carnival ride devoid of laughs but not without
grim thrills.

Almost before the wharf was out of sight, we were unanimously
seasick, and we stayed that way for most of three days. The late-year
North Atlantic has a well-deserved lousy reputation. The population
of the ship outnumbered the single johns by an outrageous ratio. We
spent woozy days and nights clinging to chains strung around large,
shallow, sloshing pools of vomitous water that would have induced
nausea even in those who felt OK. Now we had a standard against
which we could measure any subsequent peacetime discomforts,
annoyances, and frustrations. Nothing I knew could possibly be any
worse than that voyage. But after those three god-awful days, the
swells subsided and the ship steadied.

By this time, we were all ravenously hungry and, not waiting for
chow time, we rushed to the Post Exchange on board, which had re-
opened. When I got to the counter, I grabbed a whole box of
Hershey's milk chocolate bars and wolfed down all twenty-four of
them before breakfast. In my early teenage years, chocolate raised
hell with my complexion. This time nothing happened, despite the
massive Hershey's intake. I had one more teenage year to go, but I
took my still clear skin as evidence that my youth was over.

We didn't know what port or what country we were aiming for, and I couldn't even tell if we were in convoy. Once at sea, it wouldn't have made any difference whether we knew or not. But it was a first taste of an official philosophy of "What you don't know probably won't hurt you." I'm sure the idea was that later, if you were captured in combat, you couldn't reveal any secrets because you didn't know any. You could give your name, rank, and serial number as required, but that'd be all you had to give. There should probably be a statue to "The Unknowing Soldier." I remember a wartime cartoon in the *New Yorker,* in which two young women and two GIs are on a date. One of the young women is whispering to her friend, "Gee, mine doesn't know where he's been or where he's going or anything."

The lack of information, then and later, had a peculiar effect on me. Combined with the suppression of individuality during basic training, it forced me to withdraw within myself, to try to preserve some defiant, undisclosed self, some sense of privacy where no privacy was to be had. Maybe we all felt alone in the crowd. I did, and years later it struck me how few pals I'd made or kept, and how little interest I had in going to reunions.

We landed at night at Liverpool, and in the blacked-out city we disembarked onto a waiting train, the whole exercise in darkness having a kind of surrealistic quality. At one stop, motherly women appeared beside the train and offered us cups of tea, steaming and welcome in the cold air.

Our destination, it turned out, was Southampton; from there, we would cross the Channel to France. In Southampton we bunked in unheated, pyramid-shaped tents. It was said to be the coldest winter in a century and I believed it. War does that to weather somehow. By now, it was past the middle of December. What we learned only later (the private's invincible ignorance again) was that the Battle of the Bulge, that massive, last-ditch German attack, had begun on December 17th and was still raging, as the Allies mounted a counterattack.

One morning, we were rushed from our encampment to an airfield, where we clambered aboard C-47 transports. We sat there for a long time, and were then ordered off the planes again. Our places were taken by troops with battle experience who'd flown back to England for rest and recuperation. Now they were rushing back to the front. Patriotic as we were, I can't say it disappointed us not to be flying into battle. We knew how green we were.

On Christmas Eve, some of us walked into Southampton. We passed a church where we heard a congregation singing carols through a briefly opened door. I entered and stood for a moment at the back. In what I remember as a cinematic moment, I seemed to be seeing the same candles and incense and altar boys and choir that I knew from churches in Hammondsport and Camden, yet here I was in wartime England, one very homesick soldier.

The next day, we were loaded onto LSTs (landing ship tanks) in late afternoon for a night crossing to Le Havre. Not for the first time, beginner's luck saved me from embarrassment or worse. Before shipping out, we were allowed to prowl around. In the semidarkness, I kept climbing over railings across gangways to see what there was to see. When I started back, I realized that several of the LSTs must have been docked side by side perpendicular to the pier and that I must have been going from one ship to the next. Miraculously—the ships were identical—I'd returned to the right one. I might otherwise have been reported AWOL.

After the Atlantic, the English Channel was a bowl of soup, despite the season. I can't claim to have seen much of Le Havre because, again under the cover of night, we scrambled onto a long train of the same 40-and-8 boxcars in which our fathers, uncles, and perhaps grandfathers were transported to battle during World War I. The "40-and-8" stood for a car's capacity of forty men or eight horses ("*quarante hommes ou huit chevaux*"), and they made for as miserable a means of transport as they had a war ago, rough riding, paralyzingly cold, and with hardly room to stamp your feet, let alone sit or lie down.

We rolled southeast by night toward a town named Givet, on the border between France and Belgium. (Georges Simenon set one of his Maigret mysteries, *Maigret and the Flemish Shop*, in Givet, the only other time I've encountered the name.) Occasionally the train stopped and we climbed stiffly out of the boxcars and stood in line to get cans of C rations, which had been heating in hot water in fifty-gallon drums. Whatever the hour of the night, there always seemed to be gangs of kids around, begging for cigarettes and chocolate. Considering the hard time I'd had with French in college, I found it unfair that kids so young could speak it so well.

We climbed from the boxcars one last time at Givet. It was our last stop before combat.

Combat

Many years later I occasionally found myself looking into the editing rooms at movie studios, where long strips of film would be hanging from racks, their tails falling into canvas containers, waiting to be spliced together into scenes. My memories of those first weeks in combat are like those strips of film—I can no longer be quite sure what their proper order is.

From Givet, we rode for a while in Army trucks as the distant thump of artillery grew perceptibly louder. I think we walked the last little distance uphill to where L Company of the 310th Regiment of the 78th Division was encamped amid the ruins of a farm. At that point, which must have been just after New Year's Day, the "Bulge" of the Battle of the Bulge was being pushed back and reduced by the armies to the south of where we were. The 78th was helping to hold the upper end of the Allied line.

I reported to my platoon leader, a Lieutenant Miller from New York, who led me to Sergeant John Babcock, who'd just been promoted to staff sergeant in charge of the three 60 mm mortar squads. John, I soon learned, was from Ithaca, New York, where his father was a professor of farm marketing at Cornell and the founder of the Grange League Federation, which in later years became Agway. John knew Hammondsport and the wineries, and meeting him seemed then and now a wonderfully fortuitous coincidence. War was not going to be less hellish, but I no longer felt so anonymous. John was tall and lean and already showed the strain of all the action he had seen, including the first brunt of the Battle of the Bulge. He proved to be a terrific leader, calm, efficient, and steadying in all circumstances and seemingly tireless. Years later, we had a reunion in Ithaca and compared notes on our experiences in the 78th. "How was it," John said, "that a couple of innocent farm boys from upstate New York were trained to become professional killers?" He spoke with a nice touch of irony because here we were now, a retired radio-television executive and a newspaper columnist—but, once, we'd been ready to fire in earnest at those who'd been firing in earnest at us. We had been civilian soldiers greatly relieved to be nonlethal civilians again.

Back in that January of 1945, Sergeant Babcock directed me to the cellar of a barn, where I could put my sleeping bag and where I wrote some dramatic letters home by candlelight. I wish I had those letters now. I remember them as some of the most vivid and eloquent pieces I'd ever done, a little self-consciously dramatic, but I was writing from a cellar in Germany, describing the stone walls of the cellar, the straw on the floor, the sounds of the artillery overhead. I'm sure I tried to sound as if I were being brave as hell.

Once you'd been close enough to hear actual fire, you were automatically promoted from private to private first class. So I was now Private First Class Champlin.

Another of those cinematic moments flashes before me. It had thawed briefly after some intense cold, and the farmyard became a sea of mud. I was crossing it one morning when a Red Cross coffee and doughnuts jeep began backing toward me. I stood mesmerized at the sight of the two pretty American women in their Red Cross uniforms until one of them leaned out and shouted in a voice worthy of Tugboat Annie, "Get outta the effing way."

I'd learned to aim and fire the 60 mm mortar in basic training, but

I wasn't exactly friendly with it, and I quickly developed a hate-hate relationship with it. The mortar consists of three parts, the tripod, the barrel, and the baseplate, each monstrously awkward to carry. You had to lug one or another of the pieces in addition to your M-1 rifle and your backpack.

It was now late January and, in snow and occasional sleet, we moved out in pursuit of the retreating Germans. Moving out meant we began scrambling up snowy, slippery hillsides and half-stumbling, half-sliding down them, cursing the mortar all the way. The trees had all been shredded by artillery and mortar fire from the earlier fighting, and we were advancing through a landscape of desolation.

In a way, carrying a mortar piece, which was variously like lugging a manhole cover or an awkward length of pipe, helped distract me from what you might call the "outer implications." This was combat, the real thing, artillery thumping not too far off, small arms fire to be heard not too far off either. I'd have been a fool not to be scared silly. I wasn't a fool and I was truly scared, but what I felt more than anything else was an exhausted fatalism.

The Germans were in retreat ahead of us, but they were fighting a wicked delaying action. They were sniping at us from concealment every day, pinning us down with machine guns or their stuttering burp guns that fired at an incredible rate or their 88s, which whistled at us in a low and devastating trajectory. The scream of the 88s haunts me still, more than any of the other sounds of war.

The war, my war, was not quite what the movies had shown me. There was never the head-to-head slaughter of the Civil War, or the trenches, divided by no-man's-land, of the First World War. There were casualties every day, yet we (I) virtually never saw the enemy until they'd harassed us as long as they could and then surrendered. Columns of them would pass through our lines toward the rear. This was their "People's Army," the kids younger than I was and the rest, old men, Germany's last wave. They may have been relieved that their own war was over, but they were defeated and they looked it, preoccupied (I thought as I watched them) by the realization that they were in the last days of a losing war and had escaped one nightmare only to begin another. But the POWs and the occasional German corpses were all I saw of them. I also saw the extraordinarily brave medics who went out under fire to tend our wounded. At the village of Schmidt, one of the deadliest encounters on the advance, we watched as a medic struggled through deep snow to get to a wounded man. The Red Cross painted on his helmet was clearly visible, but he was dropped by a single shot from the village. Watching helplessly, I felt a surge of rage beyond anything I'd known before.

It was fighting an invisible but deadly enemy. In the official division histories, I encounter place-names—Lammersdorf, Rollesbroich, others—that we fought through. But they are a blur of cold, fatigue, and a follow-the-leader purposefulness conducted with permanently clenched stomachs because we were under fire and likely to be shot at any time.

Were we brave? Was I? Not really. Brave is when you have choices, and there weren't any realistic choices. My favorite Bill Mauldin cartoon from *Stars and Stripes* had one of his war-weary GIs, Joe or Willie, saying to the other, "What we are is fugitives from the law of averages." That was it, and the best you could do was try to bend the odds in your favor—digging your foxhole as deep as your energy would let you, keeping as alert as your fatigue would let you, keeping low so you weren't a silhouette on the horizon. We joked that it wasn't only the bullet or shell with your name on it that mattered, it was the one marked "To whom it may concern."

The luxury was sleep, any kind of sleep, anywhere. One night, I grabbed an hour or two lying on a pile of frozen turnips. I never liked turnips to begin with, but I was grateful to them on that icy night.

After days of advancing, confronting, silencing the rearguard ha-
rassers, and moving on dazed and exhausted (speaking for PFC
Champlin anyway), we paused at last just off the crest of a hill. Beyond the crest, at the foot of the hill, flowed the Roer River and a dam
that the Allies had to get control of. If it stayed in German hands,
they could presumably flood out any troops trying to move across
the river. (For once, I had an inkling of the big picture.) On the far
side of the river, the Germans were dug in, as we were on our side, all
of us for a short moment playing a wait-and-see game.

During the pause, L Company had been ordered to send a man
back to battalion headquarters for a quick course in the wiring of
field telephones. It seemed a kind of plum, as battlefield assignments
go, but it was also a chore. Sergeant Babcock gave it to me not as a
plum but because he was glad to spare his other men who'd been on
the line so long. I was really still technically a combat virgin; I'd
mostly been carrying the mortar pieces forward, like a Sherpa on an
Everest assault. We'd been moving so fast we hadn't even had time
to set up and fire our mortar. I was sure I'd never need my new
wiring skill but, as events proceeded, taking the course led to the one
solo adventure of my combat life.

Our forward squad had found a large underground cistern that
had held water for German military barracks at the foot of the hill in
the town of Blens, which was now in our hands. The squad had set
up a machine gun at the manhole that was the entrance to the concrete cave. The Germans were just across the river and the cistern
was a useful observation post as well as shelter.

One moonlit night, the sergeant woke me in my foxhole and said
that telephone communications with the cistern had been lost. Find
the problem and fix it, he said.

I started from the nearby field telephone, which the company
used to contact the bunker. When wires for field telephones were
laid, the idea was to wrap them around trees three or four times,

with plenty of slack between the trees to lessen the chance of a wire being snapped by the concussion of a mortar blast.

I picked up the wire at the phone and began tracing it, walking around and around any number of trees, a complicated procedure because each tree was apt to have more than one wire wrapped around it. Eventually I got beyond the last tree and quickly came to a flat-bottomed metal boat the Army engineers had stashed in the woods prior to the hoped-for crossing of the Roer. The rim of the boat had cut the wire like a knife.

Holding the one end of the wire I'd been following, I walked around the boat and felt along the ground for a matching wire. It was about this time that I realized I'd forgotten my carbine. I was un-armed—another interesting chapter in my unwarrior-like career. But, beginner's luck, I found the wire that led down to the bunker and, using my new talent, spliced it to the wire I was carrying. It re-mained only to make sure the connection worked. The moon was so bright I could see my shadow and, as I walked downhill toward the bunker, it occurred to me that a wakeful sniper across the river could have seen and hit me. (I'm still not sure why one didn't; maybe they were all asleep, or didn't want to start a firefight.)

I got to the bunker and nervously lifted the lid. I say "nervously" because whoever was on guard would have no way of seeing in the darkened bunker whether I was friend or foe. I whispered the pass-word, which a distant memory says was "DiMaggio." I said it sev-eral times before the sergeant in charge woke up and asked me with a snarl what I wanted. The stagnant air in the bunker smelled like last week's underwear, and the men were not so much asleep as border-ing on unconsciousness. I asked the sergeant to try phoning in. He did, and the connection worked fine. I said good night and walked back up the hill in a crouch, with many a look over my shoulder.

For my night's work, I got a half-day pass to hitch a ride into Liege, where I was able to negotiate a beer, even with my wretched

French, and saw the famous statue of the little boy peeing in the main square.

As Sergeant Babcock remembers well, that wasn't the end of my acquaintance with the cistern. A forward squad was using the abandoned German barracks at the foot of the hill in Blens. The Germans naturally had the barracks in the crosshairs of their mortars. They shelled them just as some new replacements had arrived, killing some of the new men and the company's commanding officer, who'd gone down to meet them. (My inappropriate memory is that a mortar shell hit some hot food that had been brought up by the new men, and I saw a large cannister of pancakes shredded by shrapnel.)

One of the sergeants caught some shrapnel during the barrage and was dragged to the cistern, unable to stand or walk. "You were in with us," Babcock wrote me a few months ago. "We hauled Sergeant Hogg up the steel ladder out of the cistern and, in utter darkness, one of us under each arm, started up the muddy wooded hill toward our guys, relying on your sense of direction from your messenger activities a night or two before. We were both shaking with fear, hunger, and fatigue and propelled by sporadic Bedcheck Charlie machine gun harassments."

Our yells raised some of the men in the forward foxholes at the top of the hill and they helped carry Hogg the rest of the way to the Company bunker. John remembers that, as we labored up the hill, we talked about our hopes for peacetime between gasps for breath. It was also on that climb, recalled years later, that we talked ironically about a couple of upstate lads now in the killing business.

As March began, we crossed the Roer and were within two or three days of the famous Remagen Bridge—the last one still intact over the Rhine in that area. We got to the western edge of a village named Euskirchen, where, once again, we were pinned down by heavy fire from the village.

John remembers slogging through sugar beet fields to a garage area on the outskirts. "We were lost, exhausted, and disoriented by our own big guns firing from tank destroyers behind us and zinging just over our heads," John wrote me. "The velocity of the shells could lift you off the ground. And of course the incoming noise obscured the tell-tale incoming 88s that got you."

There was still snow on the ground and a sleeting rain had begun to fall. I lay flat in an open field on the outskirts of Euskirchen, waiting for a signal to move out and trying to see through the rainwater running down my glasses. Then, as by a great wave in silent slow motion, I was lifted off the ground. I'd heard nothing, but I remember yelling, "Yahoo!" like a rodeo rider. When I landed again, I felt a kind of dull, numb pain in my right hip and I knew I'd been hit. I also realized I could no longer move my right leg.

Another sergeant ran over to me, took a look, and said, "Yeah, they got you." He carried a first-aid kit, although he wasn't a medic; he poured some sulfa powder into the wound and placed a compress on it. Having advanced to squad leader, I was wearing a .45. Just as the sergeant was about to leave—the Germans had been silenced and the outfit was moving on—he said, "Hey, we can't let the medics have this for a souvenir, and you don't need it anymore. We gotta keep it in the platoon." So saying, he unbuckled the belt and grabbed the .45. "Take it easy, the medics'll be along in a minute," he told me and ran to catch up with the others.

Several other men had been hit, some obviously worse than I had. The sleeting rain continued to fall. It grew pitch black. I could hear firing in the far distance, artillery rumbling like far-off thunder. Two of the other wounded men were moaning and calling, "Medic," in weakening voices. Now and again, I shouted, "Here!" in case the medics were searching for us in the darkness. I couldn't see my watch and I can only estimate that I lay there for about four hours. I was as scared as I ever got. No weapon. No idea when or if the medics would find me. One possibility, maybe not likely but I couldn't be sure, was that a German straggler or a German civilian might creep back and pick us off. The temperature seemed to be dropping. My hip was throbbing and I couldn't tell whether I was bleeding or not.

After what seemed a very long time, we heard American voices calling for us to yell out so we could be located. It was another surrealistic moment because you couldn't see a thing in the pitch-black night. Soon a pair of medics arrived with a stretcher, rolled me onto it, and carried me to a jeep fitted with racks. Curiously—luckily—I still felt only a dull throb in my hip. I had no feeling in my leg, but I realized I'd been lying in cold water all that time. For all my fears and dark fantasies, I felt oddly calm (in fact I seemed to be watching myself from somewhere a few feet away).

The next events, like so many, are what the movies call "jump cuts." The jeep, driving slowly over the rough ground to ease the bumps, took us to a field hospital in Aachen, where they catheterized me. I hadn't even realized it but the long lie in the wet snow had in effect frozen my plumbing, yet I'd felt no discomfort. When I saw what the procedure produced in a glass jug, it seemed a wonder I hadn't burst. The next day, I was moved by ambulance to an airfield, wearing a tag on my big toe that said, "UK by Air." In what I learned later was a C-47 transport plane fitted out with two dozen bunks, we were flown to Cheltenham and the 128th General Hospital.

Another quick cinematic moment. They've put me on the operating table to remove the shrapnel. I ask the surgeon where he went to med school.

"Harvard," he says.

"Perfect," I say, and surrender to the anesthesia.

The Summer of '46

G etting my damaged leg back to normal took several weeks pro-
gressing from crutches to a cane to walking on my own. But,
by late summer, I was pronounced fit as a fiddle and sent to duty at
the colorful old prewar Army installation of Fort Oglethorpe, Georgia. There I did personnel work, mostly steering returning GIs to
bases near their homes for discharge. I'd shot upward from private
first class to technician fifth class (T/5) or corporal, and I'd graduated from MOS (military occupational specialty) 745, rifleman, to
MOS 210, clerk.

In the early spring, one of the men in the barracks named Jack
Boyle from Auburn, New York, was on the verge of being discharged. He had his family send him his gray flannel suit, a white
button-down shirt, a red knit tie, and some brogues that bore no re-
semblance to army boots. He dolled himself up as he would look as
a civilian, and I must say it made a great impression on me. I couldn't
wait until I had the money to afford a gray flannel suit. It took me a
few years, but I finally got one and I wore it until the holes in the seat
could no longer be rewoven.

In April, I took the train back to Fort Dix, where I had started, and
was there gratefully discharged back to civilian life.

During mustering out at Fort Dix, an eager Army recruiter had
said that if I would enlist for three more years he could guarantee me

CHAMPLIN IN ARMY UNIFORM ON FENCE: *At Fort Oglethorpe, Georgia, in 1946, I was doing personnel work while I waited to be discharged. I weighed 130 pounds—but never again.*

a sergeant's stripes. I didn't believe the promise and even if it were true it was an appalling idea. Civilian life loomed like paradise. I couldn't wait.

Those last months in the Army at Fort Oglethorpe had technically been in peacetime and felt like peacetime service, with easy duty and time for play. So that getting discharged at Fort Dix wasn't exactly like being liberated from a dark cellar. All the same, it really was a liberation. No more uniform, no more saluting, no more olive drab or khaki—although, surprisingly, khaki was soon to reappear in my wardrobe.

The transition from military to civilian life was euphoric. But the euphoria was short-lived. I'd hardly gotten used to being liberated when the postwar world presented itself with all its questions: a job, income, and the longer-term questions about a career—and, in my case, the uncertainty as to whether the idea of making a living as a writer was a pipe dream.

Many of my pals in both Camden and Hammondsport had already been discharged. A few of them had gone back to their old jobs or had found new ones. But many had not and we were all members of what we called the "52-20" Club, named for the twenty dollars a week we were paid for a year by the state of New York as, I guess, a kind of mustering-out pay. The pals without jobs were temporarily discouraged about finding new ones, but we were all glad to celebrate our regained freedom.

That great miracle of the postwar era, the GI Bill of Rights, gave the prospect of a college education to millions of GIs who couldn't have dreamed of it before the war. Several of my friends, mostly those who had been in the Army Air Force and were addicted to flight, decided on careers in the service. Wedding bells did their part to break up that old gang of mine, but it was the GI Bill more than any other force that created a new future. To paraphrase a World War I lyric, "How ya gonna keep 'em down on the farm after they've seen Los

Angeles (or San Francisco or Florida or the Southwest)." One of the old gang, Bill Brady, who had been bowling with us when we heard about Pearl Harbor, became a crop duster in Louisiana.

My first stop after being discharged at Fort Dix was Cleveland to see the family. I removed the Combat Infantryman Badge and the battle stars and the medals from my uniform, tucked them into the blue case containing my Purple Heart, and placed it in one of the cubbyholes of my rolltop desk, where it still resides. I hung my uniform in a closet and never wore it again. I don't know what became of it. It may still be in a closet, now at least eight sizes too small.

I borrowed a car and drove over the hill to Camden, but my high school pals were all pretty well dispersed, although George Carle was running the family's monument works. My best girl, who had seen me through the war, was now well-advanced in her own career as a nurse and in a new romantic involvement, this time with a doctor—doctors and nurses so often finding common cause over bandages and transfusions. I viewed the change with a certain philosophical if faintly melancholy acceptance.

I was eager to get back to Hammondsport, where I hoped to spend the summer working at the family winery. By 1946, my grandmother had sold the house so full of memories at 13 Vine Street and was living in an apartment in a beautiful and historic octagonal house in Bath, New York, eight miles south of Hammondsport. The house was later torn down to make room for a surpassingly ugly three-story motel. In her apartment, my grandmother had a spare bedroom, where I could live that summer. Naturally I checked in with Uncle Charlie at the Pleasant Valley Wine Company, or "PV," as we always called it.

The winery had been part of my experience as far back as I can remember. One of my earliest memories is of a one-pound Uneeda Biscuit tin containing little metal lapel pins that I learned later read "Repeal the 18th Amendment." I didn't understand until long afterward that the 18th Amendment gave us Prohibition and that all of Hammondsport as a wine-making community was desperately eager for Repeal to end Prohibition. I just thought the little pieces of metal were interesting. As a boy, I used to ride my bicycle up to PV and visit my father's laboratory. He was the winemaker, a wine chemist by training, and his long, narrow lab with its strange odors, its glass tubing, and its Bunsen burner fascinated me. I loved to walk through the winery and to smell the heady aromas of wine fermenting in huge wooden vats more than twice my height. The wine moved from vat to vat to barrels along glass tubing, which my father had evidently helped design, and about which he wrote a scientific paper for a chemical engineering journal.

There had always been a sentimental tug to work at the winery as a career. It was pure sentiment of course. The original Charles Davenport Champlin had been the first, founding president of the winery in 1860. He had come to Hammondsport as a teenager from downstate New York and arrived to work as a clerk in a cousin's shipping office when Lake Keuka still carried a great deal of waterborne cargo. As more wineries opened in Hammondsport, the hills were covered with orderly rows of grapevines. Uncle Charlie and my father represented the third generation of Champlins at Pleasant Valley Wine Company. I would have been the fourth generation. So, in that summer of '46, I was to some extent torn between sentiment and reality. Continuity had always been important to me growing up in Hammondsport, where my personal past went back at least a century. But, just as Joe seemed destined for the priesthood from the time he was twelve, I had this compelling wish to make my way as a writer. In a sense, I split the difference that summer. I had a talk with Uncle Charlie and he agreed to take me on at the winery until I went back to college.

Somehow it was decided that I should work in the great out-of-doors as a kind of postscript to my recovery. What was available at the moment was tying grapes in the vineyards, a process by which the young vines were tied to the wires with pieces of straw using a clever knot women could do in a flash, but I had trouble mastering. So, on several spring mornings, I drove my grandmother's familiar Buick up to the vineyards and joined a small group of women, one of them a friend from high school, to tie grapes. One morning, a heavy rain drove us into a shed amid the vineyards. It was more or less dry inside, although some vines had actually grown up the shed and down from a crack in the rafters. As I sat chatting with the ladies, I looked across and saw a garden snake, which had somehow climbed up a vine and was now looking around inside. I have a deep and abiding fear of snakes, even one as young and innocent as the visitor. I yelled and ran out into the rain. I must say that, although the women were only a little calmer than I was, at least they managed their surprise a little better. I think the snake just retreated.

Because my grandmother sometimes needed the car and I had no car of my own, it was sometimes hard getting to work in the vineyards. So I changed to semi-outdoor work at the winery itself, which was easier to get to. I joined a kind of all-purpose work gang. We rode on a truck carrying cartons from a nearby warehouse to the bottling line. On one unforgettably hot day, I helped unload a boxcar of hundred-pound sacks of sugar. Some of the sacks leaked so that lugging them in the sweaty midsummer heat left us all glazed, sugar-frosted.

Then it turned out that the summer visitors had begun to arrive, wanting to tour the winery. My cousin Tony Doherty was at that point the only one in the office with time to escort visitors through, but there were more than he could handle, so I was pressed into service. For the rest of the summer, from nine until four every day, I did odd bits of typing, labels and such, in the office and took groups of visitors through the winery. I developed a wonderful spiel, some of it true. The tours ended at a reception room with heavy beams, which, I indicated, might well have come from the monastery in

France where Dom Pérignon invented champagne. Although the story had the allure of apparent truth, Tony cautioned me that this was pushing the "truth" a little too hard. The visitors all got a drink of champagne, so, from morning until afternoon, I was busy uncorking champagne, pouring, and, like a good host, having a taste for myself. Just at the end of the summer, I came down with a postgraduate cold bordering on flu. I'm afraid all those days in the penetrating coolness of a winery built back into the hills and all that champagne, excellent as it was, hadn't helped my recovery one bit.

But in the end, what marked the summer of '46 for me forever was that I fell in love. One day in late July, I'd driven to the winery in my grandmother's Buick. She'd taken the bus from Bath up to Hammondsport and we had arranged to meet at the town library after I finished work. I walked into the library, which was then in what had been one of the storefronts along Sheather Street, expecting to see my retired first grade teacher and now the town librarian, Miss Nina Arland. Instead, across from my grandmother, a pretty young woman was sitting behind the librarian's desk. I said a polite hello and escorted my grandmother to the car. As we drove away, she said that I'd been almost brusque with that nice lady. I said it had been my experience that whole summer that every woman I'd ever known was either married or engaged or hadn't liked me in any event. My grandmother, who was one of the great debriefers of all time, was able to tell me that the young woman's name was Peggy Derby and she was filling in for Miss Arland, who was ill. Peggy was in college in Georgia and lived in St. Petersburg, Florida, although her parents had had a cottage on Keuka Lake for twenty years. She had a brother John but no other affiliations so far as my grandmother knew. I confess I went back to the library the next day, took a book off a shelf, and checked it out. I then returned it the following day and checked out another book, pausing naturally to chat with Miss Derby in what was no longer even remotely a brusque way.

MY GRANDMOTHER ON THE PORCH: *My matchmaker grandmother looked like the very model of all grandmothers, petite, loyal, charming, stern if necessary, and always immensely loving. Nano's molasses cookies were the best I've ever eaten. She was lively, enthusiastic, and delightful, and I learned to drive in her 1937 Buick Century. Here she is on the porch of her apartment in Bath, where I stayed with her in the summer of 1946.*

Little did I know (and later was aghast to learn) that, during their brief conversation in the library, my grandmother had told Miss Derby the story of my pink underwear. One day, without thinking, I'd put a pair of crimson socks into the wash along with some of my white shorts and T-shirts. When these, to my embarrassment, had emerged a delicate shade of pink, it had taken more than a few washings before the color finally disappeared. Armed with probably the first nonbiographical fact she'd heard about me, Peggy, I'm happy to report, went out with me anyway.

On our first date, we went roller-skating at one of the rinks built on pilings over the lake. Nursing the bruises from our numerous falls, we had a drink afterward at the Keuka Hotel. Showing off, I ordered a Manhattan. The drink tasted awful and I never finished it, but we had a lovely conversation. We dated almost every night until I had to head for Cleveland to get ready to return to college and Peg left for the South with her family. But, as we parted, I had no doubt that this was the girl I was going to marry, whenever that became possible.

I had of course been in touch with Harvard, confirming my eagerness to return. I'd also been in touch with a friend named Joe Trowbridge, from freshman days. He lived in Newton, Massachusetts, and suggested that it would be economically prudent for me to live at his house and commute to Cambridge with him. This seemed like a better idea than it turned out to be, through no fault on the part of either Joe or his grande dame of a mother. I again felt like a bus rider, as I'd been in Cleveland; I came to see that I was missing much of the Harvard experience.

Like most other universities, Harvard was confronting some real logistical problems. The return to "regular" college life that September involved a larger than usual freshman class of men who'd been unable to start before they went in service or who were returning to finish their education. In my case, Harvard looked at the full schedule of classes I took before I left for the Army. I'd also taken a night class in Russian history while I was at Fort Oglethorpe, and they obviously pondered that, too. Then, in what I think of as a burst of cynical generosity, Harvard decided that my basic training and assorted experiences in the Army were the equivalent of a half year of college. Therefore, having left less than halfway through the first half of my sophomore year, I'd be returning to Harvard as a junior. I was so anxious to get on with my life and marry Peg that that news from Cambridge was, at first glance, wonderful. It would effectively get me out of college a year earlier than I might have expected. But, as I soon realized, there was a downside to the good news. I'd be unable to take an honors course in English, nor would there be time for all the courses I'd have to take. Here again, Harvard accommodated me. I was able to earn honors in what were called "General Studies," graduating cum laude, just on the basis of my grade point average. My entry in the Harvard alumni directories reads: "Champlin '47 cl." I'd foreshortened my Harvard experience, and I have regretted it ever since.

After I'd shown the last load of tourists through the winery and sent Peg off to Wesleyan College in Georgia, I went back to Cleveland to pack my ancient steamer trunk. Then I headed for the Trowbridge home and Harvard.

Back to Harvard

I n September 1946, instead of going to Cambridge to start my junior year, I traveled to South Station, where I was met by my new host, Joe Trowbridge, who drove me to his home at 734 Centre Street in Newton. The Trowbridge family consisted of Joe's father, Almarin, a rather crusty and eccentric stockbroker; Joe's mother, Anabel, a formidable grande dame from a strong Boston Irish family; Joe's bouncy blonde sister, Ann, who was still a student at Newton High; and Joe, himself, a Navy veteran who seldom relaxed. Almarin Trowbridge quickly persuaded me to invest some of my mustering-out pay in twenty-five shares of the Pleasant Valley Wine Company. Historically, this turned out to be a highly profitable investment, ending up as several dozen shares of Coca-Cola stock. The Trowbridge house was large, spacious, and quite splendid on a high plot above the street. In later years, as I remember, it was bought by an order of nuns.

My stay at the house got off to a jolting start. On my first Sunday morning there, we discovered that Joe's father had died in his sleep. Mrs. Trowbridge, who I thought had always run the household with quiet authority, confronted her husband's death with brave stoicism. She was now in sole command and managed all of us with a firm hand.

My cozy room on the third floor had a sloping roof and a dormer window, and I settled in quite happily. A few days after the funeral, Joe and I and Bob Carey, now back from the Marines but also intending to commute, set off in Joe's dark blue Plymouth sedan for Cambridge to enroll.

Harvard that September was in the first bloom of postwar activity. Once again freshmen were in the dormitories in the Yard. The servicemen were gone. The Navy Ensigns and their beautiful wives were, with luck, back in civilian life themselves. All the uniforms had disappeared as if by magic, except for the lingering trace of the khaki pants. The Yard and the streets around Harvard Square were crowded as all the returning veterans joined the incoming freshmen and the younger upper classmen who had missed service. The larger-than-life Daniel Chester French statue of John Harvard looked benignly down on the bustling crowd. (No one knows what John Harvard looked like, but, in gratitude for donating his whole library of two hundred volumes to the new college just taking shape in Cambridge in 1636, the officials gave the place his name.) The students hurrying among the ancient trees from Widener Library to Memorial Hall and the newer buildings beyond the Yard gave the College, or so I felt as I walked among those familiar surroundings, a different atmosphere. The population was visibly older than it'd been in prewar days and in my brief stay as a freshman. Those of us returning to pick up our studies where we'd left them were, I suspect, a majority of those enrolled. Many of the ex-GIs were married and competing with graduate students for the scarce apartments in Cambridge and in the suburbs well beyond Cambridge.

I'd spent part of my mustering-out pay on a portable typewriter I'd bought by mail from Sears Roebuck. I conclude now that it was the worst typewriter I ever owned. It was noisy; the action was slow and demanded full force from every finger. But it was a typewriter of my own and, on the fading days of summer, I would occasionally sit in the backyard at Cleveland making my first tentative stabs at writing a short story. I came up with the beginnings of a story that, many months later, I polished and sent off to one of the men's magazines. It was a thinly disguised portrait of a distant, elderly cousin of mine who'd been a race driver for a time in his youth and the racing stuff commended it to the magazine. I earned three hundred and fifty dollars and it became the first and only short story I ever sold. But, as I returned to college, I had a slightly better claim on my dreams for writing for a living.

We registered for classes, and one of my choices was a course I'd always wanted to take. It was Kenneth Payson Kempton's almost legendary course in the short story. He had published his lectures in a book entitled, fittingly, *The Short Story*. I still have it and cherish it. The difficulty was that there were several dozen of us who wanted to take the course. At the first meeting of the class, we were a standing-room-only crowd. Kempton, a slight, thin man, whose skin seemed to be stretched taut over prominent cheekbones, said that to create a realistically sized class he would give us a kind of do-or-die assignment. He commanded each of us to write two pages of fiction, two people talking, one wanting something from the other.

In a curious way, I felt that this was another crucial moment on my road to being a writer, if in fact I was ever going to make it. I went back to Newton and sat at my desk in my garret—the only appropriate setting for a young writer of course—and fed a sheet of yellow copy paper into my terrible typewriter.

What I came up with didn't really fit Kempton's specifications. I simply had my first person narrator (me, by any name) as a returning GI encountering one of the old gang from freshman year at the entrance to the Harvard Square underground. We quickly compared notes on old pals and our own military careers. I really didn't like him and resented the fact that he had had it easy in service, whereas I'd seen combat and my roommate had been killed in action. My feelings came out between the lines in a certain coolness in my talk and a certain insensitive breeziness in his chat. It wasn't all invention, of course. I'd had a confrontation like it.

Evidently, Kempton read the vibrations, the unspoken feelings, correctly and, as they say in golf, "I made the cut."

Kempton, I came to feel, was an anomaly. He was a successful commercial writer of short stories, having sold dozens of them, many to the toughest market of all, the *Saturday Evening Post*. I found his stories to be skillfully written, but far too touched with humanity to be dismissed as slick. I wondered how he got on with the academics on the faculty, who had no audiences outside of academia. When I later saw Kempton bundled up against the cold, walking across the Yard toward the classroom from wherever he lived in the suburbs, he struck me as being very much a loner.

I was one of some two dozen selected from nearly two hundred applicants. (Many were culled, but few were chosen.) It was the most significant victory on my rutted road to writerdom and, even now, I think of it with pride. I felt as if I'd climbed a rung on a ladder and had moved well beyond Hammondsport and Camden, even beyond being a Harvard freshman. I'd reached a higher level of acceptance. One of the others accepted was John P. Marquand, Jr., son of the celebrated novelist, who would later publish a novel of his own, *The Second Happiest Day*, but who spent most of his years as a magazine editor.

I worked hard on my pieces for Kempton and had relatively good luck when I tried my hand at parody or lighthearted stuff. But once, I remember, we were assigned to do a longer story, 5,000 words or more. For some reason, I decided to build a story around an anecdote one of my friends had told me about a wartime experience on a train. Although I'd had lots of wartime experiences on trains, this story hadn't happened to me and I found that I couldn't really bring it to life. When I got it back from Kempton with a C almost engraved on the cover sheet from the hard pencil he always used for comments, I found he had written down the margin of several pages, one word below another, page after page, "I know this was hard, Champlin, but this was god-awful. Serious themes are just not your dish." It wouldn't have been quite so bad if I'd disagreed with him even a little, but I knew he was right. That comment had an inhibiting effect on me for years afterward. Of necessity, though maybe also of choice, I soon abandoned fiction.

The most successful piece I did for Kempton was in fact a parody. We'd been analyzing William Faulkner's short story "A Rose For Emily." Kempton, who read one or two of our stories aloud in class each week, had one week read a piece entitled "The Fireman's Hat," by a classmate named William A. Emerson, Jr. I remember almost nothing of "The Fireman's Hat," but I somehow melded the Faulkner story and Emerson's into one rather splendidly silly pastiche, "A Fireman's Hat for Emily." The piece came back to me marked A with an asterisk, meaning return for class use. Kempton's note said, "For the small audience at which it was aimed, a masterpiece." I must say, it got a splendid laugh in the class when he read it and it confirmed his thinking and mine that serious themes weren't my dish. Another successful piece for Kempton was a parody of *Winnie the Pooh,* in which, I'm somewhat embarrassed to say now, Winnie the Pooh falls madly in love with a lady Pooh named Peggy. I managed to skate my way around serious themes in a couple of other short stories and with, I think, due credit to "A Fireman's Hat for Emily," Kempton gave me an A for the course. Though it amounted to little more than a low rung on some ladder of achievement, it had the effect of sustaining me in my thoughts of being a writer.

I was taking all the English courses I could squeeze into my schedule, including a survey of English literature given by Professor Bertram Alfred Whiting, an expert on *Beowulf* and other medieval classics. When he greeted some three hundred of us at the first session of the course, Whiting said that he and his fellow professors had kept the Harvard fires burning while we were all away, and he hoped we were properly grateful. He seemed to imply that all we'd been off doing was attending USO dances and drinking beer at the PX. But, truth be told, he did read *Beowulf* with high drama, both in modern English and in the original tongue. I can still hear his voice shouting, "Whoreson I may be, but harlot was I never."

One of my most memorable rewards for being an English major came on a spring morning in Theodore Spencer's Shakespeare course. John Gielgud was in Boston giving his one-man show "The Ages of Man," and Spencer had invited him out to talk to the class. Gielgud appeared in a tweed jacket and baggy flannel trousers, carrying a one-volume edition of the Bard in much the same manner as preachers carry a Bible. He talked a little about how he memorized words, creating visual images as ways of triggering the words. He mentioned "like Niobe, all tears" and Ruth "standing amidst alien corn." But that was really all he had to say by way of instruction. Gielgud then opened the book, or rather it seemed to fall open from long custom, to the soliloquy he was after. And he read, and read, and read, never actually seeming to look at the page. He stood motionless, not even glancing down as he turned the pages. There was only his voice, that quite extraordinary instrument, rising and falling, giving us Hamlet in triumph, Hamlet in despair, Henry awaiting the battle. It was an unbelievably moving experience—the words, of course, but perhaps even more, the magical artistry of the man saying them.

By this time, Joe Trowbridge and I had settled into a commuting routine. We'd grab what breakfast we could, dash out to the car, and, after picking up Bob Carey and a couple of other high school pals who were now also at Harvard, rush to join the morning traffic. Then there'd be the usual, desperate struggle to find a parking place and make it to class on time. I began to realize how different it was to be a commuting student, instead of a resident one. I longed to be back in Lowell House.

Having taken my faithful cornet, a King Master Model II, to Cambridge with me, in my one attempt at enjoying a real Harvard experience, I tried out for the Harvard band and was accepted. It proved to be the year that John Lardner in the *New Yorker* called the Harvard band "the best in the East." This was amazing. If Ivy League football is the most purely amateur to be found, the band was equally pure. It was run and directed by undergraduates. Unlike marching bands at the Big Ten universities, which rehearsed almost daily to work out their half-time formations of startling complexity, we had only one practice session Saturday morning before the game. How we remembered the intricate things that we did I really don't know. We ran from one formation to another, and somehow it all worked out. We did have a book full of wonderful arrangements including some medleys by Leroy Anderson, an alumnus who composed the "Syncopated Clock" and some other instrumental favorites of the day. The one peril of playing at football games was that, even in late October, you could hit a day so cold your lips would stick to the mouthpiece and the valves would literally freeze. One year, we played in the Yale Bowl, that great game always on the last Saturday before Thanksgiving. Our medley in honor of Yale appropriately included excerpts from "Rhapsody in Blue" because we were all blue with cold. On another game day, having just arrived by train from Cambridge, we marched across the Dartmouth campus in the cold light of dawn.

Every week or so, the band provided a welcome one-day respite from the curriculum. We were all under pressure to do well academically knowing that it might well help us when we started job hunting. A disproportionate amount of my time was spent at the noisy portable, doing my pieces for Kempton. I didn't begrudge a minute of that time, although occasionally, in the wee hours of the morning, I'd fall asleep with my head on the typewriter.

I am still grateful to Kenneth Kempton for his encouragement, even in the face of my troubles with serious themes. When I graduated in 1948, I asked Kempton for a letter of recommendation. In his most gracious reply, he said he'd be delighted to write such a letter, and he sent one right along, although I never had occasion to show it to anyone.

Well before June, I'd realized full well that I was missing too much of the Harvard experience by commuting from Newton. The tyranny of the traveling to and from Cambridge was frustrating even though Joe, his sister Ann, and Joe's mother, Anabel, were wonderfully hospitable. I think even Joe recognized that I was growing restless. We were coming up to the end of term, when I would have to decide what to do next. Fred Herberich, a prelaw major from Akron and another friend from freshman days, said he'd be glad to have me as roommate at his quarters back in Lowell House. I sent my trunk to the storeroom at Lowell and went back to spend another summer as a tour guide at the winery.

The Last Keuka Lake Summer

The drill at Harvard was to put a self-addressed postcard in your final exam book. The professor would indicate your grade so that the news, good or bad, could follow you home. I discovered that the A I'd extracted from Kempton had put me on the dean's list.

I'd arranged to spend a second summer working as a tour guide at Pleasant Valley, but Uncle Charlie knew that joining the winery permanently wasn't on my agenda. He wrote me an understanding letter in which he said he knew that people in journalism were wedded to it. He said "journalism" instead of "writing," although, at that point, I couldn't be sure that I'd end up in journalism.

Knowing that the winery was only a temporary occupation for me that summer, I was not free of angst. What the future held wasn't clear. Graduate school? Freelance writing? A job? Marriage was the most attractive possibility, but, for the moment, it was out of the question financially.

As I went back to the wine cellar, I had no idea how short a time it would be before the forces of change were to affect the winery forever. Whatever sentimental pull I felt about being a part of the Pleasant Valley Wine Company, the tug of the typewriter was even stronger. I knew that I was living the last months of my working attachment to PV, which had been part of my experience for as long as I could remember.

Three years later, in 1950, Uncle Charlie Champlin would die of a sudden and unexpected heart attack. He was succeeded as president by Bob Howell, a retired Hammondsport coal and lumber dealer and a cousin by marriage. After Bob Howell's brief tenure, Thomas Holling, a former mayor of Buffalo representing various shareholders, took over for a while. PV had been a publicly held corporation since floating a stock issue just after Repeal to raise capital for resuming production. Subsequently the winery was bought by an entrepreneur from New York named Marne Obernauer, who in time sold his controlling shares to the Taylor Wine Company next door. Taylor and PV, now a subsidiary, were then bought by Coca-Cola for reasons that were never really clear because Coke did nothing to promote the wineries, whose sales dried up almost completely. Coca-Cola dealt the wineries off to Seagram, which did nothing except manufacture some wine coolers, then in vogue. After Seagram, a management group took over and tried unsuccessfully to revive the wineries. Then the physical properties were bought by Mercury Aircraft, a strong, prosperous, and locally owned metalworking firm there in Hammondsport.

But all those dark and depressing times for both PV and Taylor lay some years ahead. In the summer of 1947, I was delighted to be back in what felt like the bosom of my corporate family.

I was the only full-time guide that summer. If we acquired an overload of visitors, cousin Tony Doherty would take a party out himself. Postwar tourism was only beginning to get under way. As it grew, PV took on several guides. The larger Taylor winery next door had something like four dozen guides and a tourist center on the valley flatland below the wineries.

I met my tour groups in the lobby and led them up the stairs, past Uncle Charlie's office on their right and down a corridor that led to the working winery and its huge vats, in which the grape juice fermented with wonderful, heady aromas.

In his own early days at the winery, Tony was assigned to clean one of the empty vats. Having crawled into the vat the usual way, through a kind of large bunghole at the bottom, he soon passed out from the lingering fumes. It would have been curtains for him except that one of the other workmen, nervous that Tony's feet had gone still, had pulled him out.

As a tour guide, I was aware that the main reason people wanted to tour the winery was to get a taste of champagne at the end. But I thought it only right that they should pay for their sip of champagne by listening to my spiel as we toured the premises. Actually I have always found the making of "real," as opposed to bulk-processed, champagne fascinating because the process has changed so little over the years since Dom Pérignon invented the beverage three or four centuries ago at the old Abbey of Hautvillers, where he was cellar master. The making of the best champagne was labor intensive then, and it still is today.

As I told the visitors, it all begins with the cuvée, a careful blending of white wines that give a champagne its distinctive flavor. The cuvée is placed in the heavy, dark bottles where it will spend the rest of its life until it is joyously consumed. A mixture of yeast and sugar is added, to produce the fermentation that makes the champagne bubbly. The bottles are placed in tiers in the subterranean vault, the thousands of bottles laid horizontally in layers higher than a man's head.

I liked to pass along the story, which I was told as true, that in the old days, when champagne making was an almost mystical art, the pressure of the carbon dioxide released by the fermentation would cause some of the bottles to explode like gunshots. The vaults could sound like a shooting gallery, with the smell of wine heavier than ever and the floors littered with shards of glass. According to family legend, great-uncle Victor, a graduate chemist out of Lehigh University, took the guesswork out of the mix of yeast and sugar. He became a champagne consultant to several wineries in Hammond-sport and elsewhere.

Once the fermentation is complete, I told my parties, the bottles are placed neck down in A-frame racks. Each day, ambidextrous men called "riddlers" lift each bottle and give it a quarter turn. Eventually the dead yeast collects on the cork. The bottles are then carefully transferred, still neck down, into a brine solution that freezes the wine about an inch from the cork.

Now a brave and skillful man called the "disgorger" takes a bottle; working inside a kind of keg with an open side, he pries off the staple that holds the cork in place. The pressure in the bottle blows out the cork, the ice, and the sediment. The disgorger puts the bottle on a nipple which restores the lost wine. The bottle is given a permanent cork and the famous wire hood.

It's interesting to note how much the local industry has changed since I was giving my spiels over fifty years ago. All of the wines that Pleasant Valley made at that time had what were essentially European titles—sauternes, Tokays, ports, and sherries. Theoretically the PV champagne ought not to have been called "champagne" because the name was presumably reserved to the sparkling wines from the Champagne district of France around Epernay. But custom brought champagne to the United States and custom keeps the name in use. Pleasant Valley is in fact still "U.S. Bonded Winery No. 1" and, so far as I know, was the first producer of champagne in the United States.

Another legend, with currency even beyond the family, is that in the early days of the winery, great-grandfather Champlin took a case of the champagne to Boston in hopes of making a customer of the great New England provisioner, S. S. Pierce (pronounced "perse"). Marshall Wilder, the president of the firm, offered chilled glasses of the wine to his board of directors, and announced that "Gentlemen, this is some champagne wine from the great western part of our country." Champlin realized that he'd just heard a wonderful brand name for the champagne, and it has been called "Great Western" ever since, and is to this day.

Sadly enough, so I strongly feel, of the three largest of the Hammondsport wineries—Taylor, Pleasant Valley, and Gold Seal, which was north along Keuka Lake at Urbana—only Pleasant Valley struggles on in Hammondsport, leased to Michael Doyle, a local lawyer who first came to town as a Taylor executive. But, in place of the large wineries, there are literally dozens of "boutique wineries," as they are called, scattered throughout the hills that line Keuka and the other Finger Lakes, and they make their wines from a great number of new hybrid grapes. Many of the new wines take frequent prizes in competitions here, and even abroad.

I finished my work as a tour guide, having, I thought hopefully, created dozens of new customers for Great Western champagne. But the end of that summer had a curious feeling of closure in many ways. Although the last three of Jules Masson's children, my great-aunts Julia, Matilda, and Josephine, still lived in the large house he'd built across the street (they are now all gone, and the house with its grounds covering almost a square block has changed hands several times), my grandmother's house on Vine Street had been sold a few years before. And although the band concerts in the park still existed, I was no longer tootling with them as I had with such extravagant pride when I was fourteen or fifteen. The Park Theater was no more—nor indeed was the Hammondsport of my childhood and adolescence. Postwar Hammondsport was still beautiful and, in a curious way, it was still my home away from home, and yet I was a visitor.

If the summer of 1946 had been a kind of joyous return to civvies, civilian life, and freedom after the regimentation of the military, the summer of 1947 was a kind of punctuation in my life, a closure—but also a commencement. Peggy had already lined up a job at the Winthrop-Stearns Research Institute in Rensselaer, New York, to begin in September; she'd made arrangements to room in nearby Albany with Marjorie Walton, a high school friend of mine from Camden. I was, of course, going back to Harvard for my last year. I had mixed emotions about that.

My thoughts about writing had been dwelling upon journalism as a possible avenue for me. My new idols among writers now included A. J. Liebling, whose own writing about the war in North Africa, boxing, food, and the ills and sins of newspaper journalism itself I found admirable and enthralling. All the wartime coverage by many hands made a deep impression on me. Liebling, E. B. White, and the other *New Yorker* writers were writing out of their own personal experience. Increasingly, it was experience that I could not only understand but, to some extent, share. For the first time, I felt I had experiences worth writing about. More and more, instead of fiction, expository writing presented itself as the likely wave of my future.

Farewell, Fair Harvard

As a man whose mother preserved his fourth grade report cards for years (all A's but imperfect attendance because of the usual childhood diseases), I probably inherited the same ever-keeping tendency. When the report cards surfaced somewhere, I tossed them out with the greatest reluctance, if only because they were signed by Miss Florence Gordon, one of the loveliest and most soft-spoken of my grammar school teachers. But, for all my preservative tendencies, I have been unable to find any of my Harvard course lists. A couple of the printed hour exams, with obviously feverish notes to myself in the margins as I scrawled away furiously in the exam blue books—I can't find any of those either.

The point is that I can only remember two of the courses I took that last year at Harvard. One produces the occasional remembered amusing line; the other was memorable and life changing. The one was a survey course in poetry conducted by Harry Levin, a well-known expert on James Joyce and a lecturer of exceptional polish. No word he spoke in my hearing ever sounded extemporaneous, not even remotely spontaneous. My most vivid memory is of the day when he announced, "Today I shall take up the Cavalier poets, which I intend to treat in cavalier fashion."

The other was a writing course I took in my last term from a tall, slender, elegant, and urbane (but spontaneously urbane) man named Carvel Collins. He looked as if he could have stepped out of a Scott Fitzgerald novel or could play Fitzgerald in a film. He was also leading Harvard's first seminar on the work of William Faulkner, whom he knew and on whom he was a recognized authority. I'd had to beg my way into Collins's class because it was essentially an optional English class for lowerclassmen only. But I was an upperclassman, one desperate to take another writing course, and one not encumbered by the obligations of an honors program.

Not being an honors candidate in English was a mixed and as I came to feel dubious blessing for me. Having essentially telescoped my sophomore year into a few hurried weeks before I went into the Army, I came back as an entering junior.

So, there, in my last term at Harvard, Carvel Collins took pity on me and let me join the class. It was a heavenly writing course. Collins demanded only a thousand words a week, in any form: short story, essay, review, chapters of a novel, or each in turn as the weeks went by. I think my first paper for him was a critique of *Gentleman's Agreement*, which starred Gregory Peck as a Gentile posing as a Jew to expose anti-Semitism in upscale hotels and resorts. It was a fairly daring film for a Hollywood not much given to tough social realism. I admired the film and its intentions; Collins admired my piece. Although, in hindsight, it's easy to say that I was pointing to a later career as a film critic, I don't think that's true. In high school, I once wrote a parody film review that began, "Of all the thousands of films that have flickered and danced before these tired eyes. . ." I don't think that was an instinctive prophecy either. It was just that, like everyone in my generation, I grew up on the movies and they were part of my psyche.

I took full advantage of the freedom of form and topic that was possible in Collins's class. I wrote a few memoir pieces (an early habit) and a few book and author appreciations (another early habit). I wrote some semi-fictional vignettes drawn from incidents in my life in and around Lowell House. They were moments rather than stories, summonings of atmospheres and attitudes. Collins liked these particularly, and his penciled notes, scrawled on the smeary erasable paper, urged me each time to think about a novel in which, he said, such vignettes would fit perfectly. The idea of a novel was extremely tempting, and I regret to this very day that I never undertook to write one. The nearest I've come to fiction, except for the one short story I published early on, is to consciously use some of the techniques of fiction in reporting—describing character and settings, capturing action.

On the home front, I'd moved to Fred Herberich's suite in F entry of Lowell House. Fred was a quiet-voiced scholar on his way to law school and a career as a tax and estate expert with a Boston firm. We were congenial roommates and remained friends, although we only met at class reunions. Fred was a devout Christian Scientist. By this time, I was hanging on to Catholicism by my fingertips, an intermittent attendee to say the most.

I have one searing memory of my first days rooming with Fred. It was a football weekend, the Dartmouth game as I remember. I had no date (Peg was not with me) and I was feeling ever so slightly sorry for myself. I partied with some friends after the game, partied too well, and because I usually drank so sparingly, I felt suddenly unwell. I dashed back to Lowell House and burst into the room, where Fred and his date and one or two other couples had gathered before going off to a dance. The women each looked more scrubbed and virginal than the other and the men were, like Fred and the girls, all nondrinkers. I dashed past them all, waving but wordless, and rushed into the bathroom. Fred swiftly and kindly shut the door behind me. Although I turned on both faucets and flushed the toilet, I knew full well that some of my ghastly retching sounds would be entirely audible in the living room. In a moment of respite, I thought I heard some girlish giggles, then Fred said, "See you later" and they left. I'm not sure we spoke of it the next day at all. But I am sure that my performance left Fred with his own theological and behavioral beliefs more deeply ingrained than ever.

I was still hammering out my stories and class assignments on my slow-motion portable. Fred had a much better portable, a Smith-Corona, I think, and I borrowed it whenever he wasn't using it because I could write twice as fast on it. Graduation was still a matter of a few months away, but the years beyond it—the matter of a job— loomed larger. Late in the winter, Harvard organized a "Journalism Day" for anybody curious about working in that field. I went along. The guests of honor were that year's Nieman Fellows. I had a long talk that afternoon with a slim, bespectacled young man who was the labor columnist for the *Chicago Sun-Times*. He was Robert William Glasgow, and our paths were to cross later. I'd begun to think about the possibility of graduate studies in journalism. Beyond graduation, I still had some benefits left under the GI Bill. During spring vacation, I called Syracuse University, whose Newhouse School of Journalism was excellent. I was told that I'd have to take some undergraduate courses at Syracuse before I could enter the graduate program. That ended my thoughts about graduate school.

The writing I did for Carvel Collins was the most satisfying part of my senior year, and, as things turned out, the most consequential. When Collins returned my last paper for the course, I found a longer than usual note at the bottom of the last page. He told me that he'd had a note from an editor at *Life* who was looking for writers and who would be glad to consider anyone Collins cared to recommend. In his note, Collins freely offered to do so for me. Since I didn't have a glimmer of a job, I eagerly accepted his offer. Wondering aloud why anyone would want to write those little captions in the magazine, Collins said with a smile, "Let's go over to my office and write a letter." And so we did. As I remember, the letter was enthusiastic without being effusive. It emphasized my writing skill and tactfully did not mention my almost total lack of journalistic experience. I'd always been in awe of *Life* magazine and without undue modesty could frankly say that I didn't think I had a chance of even being called for an interview. But, very shortly, I got a letter from James Crider of *Life,* inviting me to New York for a meeting.

A year earlier, the Class of 1947 Commencement speaker, General George C. Marshall, had used the occasion to enunciate what became known as the Marshall Plan for the reconstruction of Greece and Turkey and indeed all of Europe. Despite my two years in the Army, I was graduating in 1948 as a member of the Class of 1947. Graduation turned out to be on the date Crider now proposed for our interview. I could have put off my New York trip for a day or two, but I didn't dare let the magazine think that I'd play fast and loose with their wishes. I never told Crider I was skipping graduation.

I said good-bye to Fred, went home, packed an overnight bag, and then took a train to New York. As the comedian Mort Sahl would remark in a later album, "The future lies ahead." I wasn't at all sure that it did, but, at that moment, it was at least a possibility.

Intimations of Life

I n 1948, *Life* magazine had the largest circulation of any weekly magazine in the country, with something approaching seven million copies weekly and three times that many readers. Its cover design, white letters in a red box, was familiar virtually everywhere on earth. Many of the *Life* photographers, like Margaret Bourke-White, Robert Capa, and Alfred Eisenstaedt, had celebrity status. The magazine's photographs and stories themselves often made news.

The great general circulation magazines like the *Saturday Evening Post* and *Colliers* commanded wide audiences of their own. The print magazine field hadn't yet begun to feel the competition from television for advertising revenue that would within two decades seal their fate.

In 1948, daily television broadcasting in the United States was only a few years old. As an idea, television had been around for a long time. Milton Berle later remembered doing experimental television transmissions in the late 1920s, wearing green makeup because the primitive cameras couldn't record flesh tones accurately. As early as 1936, both German and British (BBC) television had begun daily broadcasts. The Germans televised the 1936 Olympics. In the United States, by 1942, experimental licenses had been granted to eighteen stations, but World War II put a stop to the development of the medium of television. At the end of the war, however, television was in the wings, a potential giant waiting to be born. The early tele-vision programs were all black and white. Until the coaxial cable linking New York and Los Angeles was completed, viewers west of Chicago could see national programs only via what were called "kinescopes," made by filming monitor screens and so deficient in detail and contrast that they brought to mind one critic's joke about the photographs in the Paris *Herald* in the 1920s, which "looked as if they had been engraved on pieces of wet toast." The appeal of televi-sion was obviously enormous and growing, and the number of sets in use was rising very fast.

But, for the moment, the supremacy of print journalism wasn't yet seriously challenged, and on a morning in early June, I was call-ing on *Life* magazine. I'd booked a room at the Manhattan Towers hotel, attracted by a lush piece of popular music that bore its name. I walked from the hotel to the Time-Life building at 9 Rockefeller Plaza, but I was still early, so I went around the corner to a Child's restaurant on Fifth Avenue and hunched over a cup of coffee, killing time. To my surprise, Bill Emerson, the classmate from Kempton's short story course, whose piece I had parodied, was sitting there nursing his own cup of coffee. We didn't really know each other well, but now we had common cause. He said he was waiting to see Max Gissen, who was the book critic and, I think, a senior editor of *Time*. I said I was going to see Jim Crider at *Life*. There was a nuance here. Seeing a recruiter for *Life* was not quite the same, not quite as distinguished, as seeing one of the top editors at *Time*. I was eager for whatever *Life* would ask me to do. Bill explained that he was only in-terested in being assigned to *Time*'s Atlanta bureau. He lived in Georgia. In the end, *Time* didn't give him Atlanta, but *Newsweek* did; he was to end his magazine career as the last editor of the old *Satur-day Evening Post*.

Bill and I wished each other luck and I took the elevator to the 31st floor and asked my way to Crider's office. Curiously, Crider seemed from exactly the same mold as Carvel Collins, almost a twin. He wore a gray flannel suit. He had thinning blond hair and he was both casually and elegantly handsome in a way that hinted of Scott Fitzgerald, even as Collins did. He was a gracious and charming host to a nervous job applicant; in the years to come, he became a good friend and an editorial colleague in the Chicago office. Just now, he walked me around the 31st floor and down an interior stairway. The 31st was the news floor and Crider introduced me to various dignitaries, including his immediate boss, Wilson Hicks, the executive editor of the magazine. Hicks glanced at my résumé as I sat there, grunted a hello, and thanked me for stopping by. If he asked a question, I have no recollection of what it was. Down the hall, we met Marian MacPhail, who was the head of *Life*'s researchers. She was the daughter of the baseball magnate Larry MacPhail; like Crider, she later became and remained a close friend all of her days. Marion asked me several questions, mostly along the lines of what I hoped to do at the magazine. I said I hoped to write, not explaining further that it was all I knew how to do. I was aware that I was balefully ignorant of how the magazine was organized and precisely how and where the writers fit in.

There was one moment that was to trouble me for quite some time. On our tour, we passed an office where a man sat bent into his typewriter amid a halo of cigar smoke. Jim shook his head as we passed and said, quite indiscreetly I thought, that the writer hadn't had a raise in some time but didn't seem to get the message. I thought to myself, oh, great, they don't fire you; they just don't give you raises and let you figure it out for yourself. Later on, when I'd somehow become a trainee, I worried incessantly about raises. It cost me some sleep.

Crider's tour took most of the morning. He told me how to claim for the train fare and the hotel room and said in the time-tested manner of employers always, "Don't call us, we'll call you." I thought I'd been polite but less than compelling all morning, and I knew in my heart of hearts that I was unlikely ever to hear from the magazine again.

Back at home, my stepfather and I began casting about for ideas that might lead to employment. I'm not sure how he got wind of the job, but he learned that there was an opening for a beginning reporter on the Cortland, New York, *Daily Standard*. Cortland was and is a prosperous and very Republican community in a lush dairy region southeast of Syracuse. The *Daily Standard* was accordingly a prosperous and very Republican newspaper.

Pop and I drove over to Cortland one day and met the editor. It all seemed too easy to be true. The editor would be delighted to have me on staff and could pay me thirty dollars a week for the first year, with an increase to $32.50 the second year. He would give me a gift subscription to the paper so I could familiarize myself with the city officials and other citizens likely to fall under my eye as a reporter. Cortland was a long way from 9 Rockefeller Plaza, and although Crider and I had never come close to discussing money, I sensed the pay might be better in Manhattan. But at least I had a job to start on the first Monday in August 1948. Peggy and I subsequently made our own trip to Cortland. The local public library offered to employ her at least part-time, and we found a small, clean room and bath we could rent. We figured to get married as soon as possible after I started work.

And there it stood. Then, after a month of silence, I had a call on a Wednesday from Jim Crider, who asked me if I could come back down to New York the next day because there were those at the magazine who wanted to sniff at me again. No overnight stay this time. I took an early train to the city and saw Crider in the afternoon. It was oddly like a replay of the first visit. Hicks grunted and Marian was very nice and I caught a train upstate later in the afternoon, wondering if that trip had been necessary. Well, it had been. Crider called me

FAMILY AT THE TABLE: *Taken with the self-timer in the kitchen at Cleveland—a Sunday probably, with Pop dressed for church, Peg and I at his left, Nancy and Nano with their backs to the camera. Joe is at the end, at left, with Mother and Pop looking uncomfortable, as they always did in the presence of the camera.*

promptly on Friday morning and said, could I please report for work Monday morning at a salary of $50 per week. It was an extraordinary day and a tumultuous weekend. Mother had been in Syracuse for some tests and the reports had come back that she had uterine cancer. My sister, Nancy, turned five, and Joe was off to Yale. And I had two jobs, both starting Monday morning. Pop and I arranged to meet the editor in Cortland on Saturday and we drove over to see him, both of us with tears in our eyes and saying very little. I must confess that the editor couldn't have been kinder. He said that he couldn't think of standing in the way of my job at *Life*. I'd of course had a moral commitment to take the job, but now I was released.

Back in Cleveland, I realized painfully that the burden of helping Mother through the cancer therapies must fall heavily on Pop, although I'd come back up from New York as often as I could. Fortunately, Mother was to conquer this invasion of cancer and return to her old life—as I was starting my new one.

On Sunday, Mother and Pop drove me to the train. I checked into the Manhattan Towers Hotel again and, on Monday morning, reported to Jim Crider to begin work at *Life*.

Luce

W hen I joined Time, Inc., as a twenty-two-year-old trainee in August 1948, Henry Robinson Luce—the remarkable journalistic entrepreneur who founded *Time, Fortune* (a daring gamble in the depths of the Depression; a business magazine costing a dollar a copy), *Life,* and *Sports Illustrated*—was at the height of his powers. He was very rich and very influential, acknowledged all over Western civilization as an opinion holder and opinion maker.

I'm not sure when I first caught sight of this intense, gray figure, possibly at the elevator bank off the lobby. There were elevator starters in those prosperous days and when one of them saw Luce coming, he kept lesser passengers at bay, saving the elevator for Luce, who then ascended alone to his office on the 33rd floor. One of his biographers, W. A. Swanberg, said that Luce acknowledged using the elevator ride to say his daily morning prayer. But Luce often came back down to the 31st floor, where *Life* had its editorial offices, to consult with the managing editor, then Edward K. Thompson, on the cover choices for the next week and possibly beyond, to discuss major story assignments, and on most days items of opinion and potential controversy. *Life* had an editorial writer—two in fact—and the chief writer, John Knox Jessup, was often waiting for Luce when he arrived for sessions with Thompson. For the editorial writers, Jessup and his second-in-command, William Miller, it was not unlike waiting for the voice of God.

I sometimes passed Luce as he emerged from a "down" elevator on the 31st floor, head bent as if in deep concentration, wearing one of the gray suits he almost always wore. He was slim and trim, his hair graying and thinning on top, although his eyebrows were at least as bushy as those of the controversial labor leader John L. Lewis. He loved to stand around quietly while Thompson was looking at pictures and laying out a story.

Now that Time, Inc., is only a cog (though a highly profitable cog) in a muddled conglomerate, it is nostalgic to look back to the decades when *Time was* Henry Luce.

Luce and his partner, Briton Hadden, had founded *Time* on a proverbial shoestring in 1923. Hadden had intended to be the editorial side of the magazine; Luce, the business side. But Hadden died in 1929, just after his thirty-first birthday, and Luce carried on alone, overseeing both business and editorial matters, with a great deal of help on the business side from the magazine's first executive employee, Roy Larsen.

The fiscally courageous decision to start *Life* and later *Sports Illustrated* spoke both to Luce's business acumen and to his daring as a risk taker. *Life* was famous for nearly having foundered at its birth, its ad rates set far too low in light of the magazine's extraordinary newsstand sales. The production costs far outweighed the revenues until the ad rates could be adjusted significantly upward. The initial rate card became a collector's item.

Sports Illustrated and its attention not just to the behemoth sports like baseball and football but to specialty and minority enthusiasms like archery, fencing, court tennis, and track had been Luce's ideas. The magazine lost money for ten years, but Luce stuck with it, against some kindly advice from his colleagues, until it turned the corner and became, with *Time* itself, Luce's and his corporation's prodigal gold mine.

In his remarkable *New Yorker* profile of Luce in the late 1930s, Wolcott Gibbs told of one of Luce's classmates at Yale who saw Luce walking across the campus, head bowed in deep concentration. "Careful, Harry," the classmate yelled after him, "you'll drop the world." The profile, in not kindly but awed tones, prophesied that the end of young Luce's remarkable power and wealth was not yet. Luce was in fact an influence in Republican Party circles because of the presumed importance of what *Time* and the other magazines said about issues and candidates. But *Time*'s avowed Republican bias could do little for Landon, Wilkie, Dewey, or indeed any other Republican. It was FDR's and the Democrats' time.

Luce obviously lived by passionate convictions, including, as he once said, his "invincible Protestant ignorance," an ironic acknowledgment that his closest friends included the celebrated Jesuit preacher and writer John Courtney Murray and the Protestant theologian Reinhold Niebuhr. His other passions included Yale, conversation, the World Council of Churches, and the Republican Party. One of the stories I loved about Luce was that, at a luncheon meeting with the editors, he spoke in what became an exceedingly long monologue while the editors had drinks, the main course, and dessert. "Well," said Luce, as he finally finished speaking, "shall we eat now?"

The rise of John F. Kennedy posed a dilemma for Luce. He and Joseph P. Kennedy were old friends. So, for that matter, were Luce and JFK. Luce had written the introduction for JFK's first book, *While England Slept*, inspired by the young Kennedy's time in London while his father was the ambassador to the Court of St. James on the eve of World War II.

When Kennedy was nominated for president, Luce told a gathering of *Time*'s senior editors that their coverage of the campaign should be played (as one of those present told me) "right down the middle." To which, my source also told me, one of the *Time* editors, exclaimed, "Harry, what a great idea!" Then Luce, who'd been only twenty-five when he started *Time* in 1923, announced that he wasn't going to hang on as a gray eminence in the tradition of other press barons like William Randolph Hearst. He and his controversial out-spoken wife, Clare Boothe Luce, retired to a compound in Arizona and there he died, on February 28, 1967.

His executive technique had been to have two or three editors, sometimes even more, all aspiring to reach the top at the same time. The competition was fierce, if usually discreet. One of *Time*'s best assistant editors with justified aspirations to be the editor, but who didn't make it, famously cabled Luce, "Why did you keep me under the mistletoe if you weren't going to kiss me?" Luce's system, often cruel in its workings out, did produce a robust crop of talent, chief among which was Henry Anatole Grunwald; born in Vienna, Grun-wald rose from office boy to be the editor-in-chief of all the Time, Inc., magazines (in succession to Luce himself).

Whenever Luce visited a city where there was an editorial bureau, he usually arranged to have luncheon or dinner with the staff. He was famous all his days for his almost obsessive curiosity—about the city, about rents, about the local pols, about everything. When he arrived at a bureau city, the bureau chief was usually called upon to meet him at the airport and ride with him to his hotel. For some of the less secure bureau men, this was something of an ordeal. While waiting for Harry, Denver man Barron Beshoar once made a dry run along the route from airport to hotel, scanning the scenery on both sides of the highway in a desperate attempt to figure out what questions Luce might ask. As it happened, Luce demanded to know the names of each of the Rocky Mountain peaks he could see from the limo. Beshoar glibly reeled them off, one after the other. Later on, he confided to a close friend that he knew the names of almost none of the peaks, but he'd given them the names of the north-south running streets in North Denver, which he did know. Luce, in turn, told others how extraordinary it was for Beshoar to know the name of every mountain peak in Colorado.

One of the innumerable Luce legends involved a Los Angeles bureau man who had to accompany Luce on a car ride from Los Angeles to San Francisco. Long before the limo reached San Francisco, the man had run out of answers. At one point, they drove past a large excavation. "What's that?" Luce asked. Figuring all was lost anyway, the bureau man answered, "That's a hole in the ground, Harry."

The truth was that Luce had insatiable curiosity. He usually came back from any trip with memos for his editors, individually or collectively. Another of the legends is that, returning from an early postwar flight across the country, Luce sent out a memo that said simply, "Roofs." He'd been impressed by the sheer volume of new home construction he'd seen below him. Whether one of the shorter-lived Time, Inc., magazines, *House and Home,* grew out of that observation I don't know. But I wouldn't be surprised if it did.

On one of his last official visits to Los Angeles (where I was, by then, working in the bureau), he had a quiet dinner with some of us in what was known as the "upper room" at Perino's, then the fanciest restaurant in town. Two items from that evening are still vivid in my memory. The bureau included a young and outspoken man, Bob Jones, recently arrived from the University of Wisconsin, long known for its passionate liberalism. It turned out that both Luce and Jones had recently read the same book on the origins of World War I. They disagreed on its thesis, and Bob was soon pounding the table and saying things like "Damn it, Harry, that's nonsense!" Never a man to ripple the calm surface of things, the bureau chief could be seen to be dying inwardly; time and again, he tried to break in and deflect the contentious discussion. But he hadn't reckoned with Henry Luce. Luce turned to him and said, "Are you trying to end my conversation with this fascinating young man?" When that conversation finally did wind down, the bureau chief turned to Luce and said, "Harry, what effect do you think [Nelson] Rockefeller's divorce will have on his political career?"

Once described as being so voluble he sometimes had trouble finishing a complete sentence (I often thought he spoke like a man dictating cablegrams), Luce answered, and here I quote almost verbatim: "I was in Delhi. World Council of Churches. One day, they suggested I see some ruins a hundred and fifty miles south of Delhi. Well, you know what it's like in Delhi. Imagine what it's like a hundred and fifty miles south. But I went. Knew the ruins would be third rate and they were. My driver and I were having lunch at some hostel. His name was Krishna something. Not Krishna Menon, but there are a lot of Krishnas over there. So Krishna, whatever his name was, said, 'Mr. Luce, what effect do you think Rockefeller's divorce will have on his political career?' Well! What divorce? Read four papers a day. Thought I was well informed. Asked Krishna how he knew. Said he read it in the *International Herald-Tribune*. Where was his copy of the paper? Back at his hovel in Delhi. So we drove back to Delhi and I read the paper and sure enough the divorce was announced by Rockefeller's lawyer, Maurice T. (Tex) Moore. My brother-in-law! Married to my sister, Beth. Had dinner with Tex and Beth the night before I left and he didn't say a word about the divorce. Had a letter from Beth a couple of days later and she said she told Tex he should have tipped me off about the divorce. But Tex said, no, the client relationship was sacred. So I became the last person in the world to hear about Rockefeller's divorce."

I suspect there was an earlier point in his career when a situation like that would have stirred Luce to outrage, but mellowness had come to him, as it must to all men, and he didn't mind saying the joke was on him.

Good timing has always been part of my luck. I was lucky to come to work at *Life* magazine when it was at the height of its power and prestige, and only a little while before it all began to change, as television continued its skyrocketing rise to its own power and prestige. I was also lucky to work at *Life* in the time of Luce himself, when the whole corporation still seemed to be summed up in the personality of its remarkable founder, Henry R. Luce.

The Future Begins

I'd had, I realized later, only a breather from war. The postwar years had all too briefly carried an aura of peace and what promised to be normalcy. The Cold War was upon us. In 1948, the Russians were blockading Berlin and the United States had organized a massive airlift to get supplies to the beleaguered city. It wouldn't be long before the Chinese Communists would push Chiang Kai-shek off the Chinese mainland and onto Taiwan. There were war clouds in the sky, even as there had been most of my early life. Heading for my first job in New York City, I was admittedly far more conscious of my own life and future than of the geopolitical realities of the world, but first things first.

When I arrived for work that first day at 9 Rockefeller Plaza, I had no idea what Jim Crider and the others saw in me. As I came to realize, they must have considered me something of a lump, beautifully free of preconceived ideas, one that could be molded into the form that worked best for *Life*. As I also came to realize, my timing was perfect. In its confident expansion in those early postwar years, *Life* took aboard staff at a rate it never would match again, and the generation that was hired from the late 1940s to the early 1950s was essentially the crew that took *Life*—as a weekly—to its heights, then saw it through its decline and laid it to rest at the end of 1972. In its final years, *Life* would have a brief, forlorn coda as a monthly (with the impact, I'd always think, of a tin candy box) after I'd gone on to other pursuits. The magazine would finally be reduced to special issues, books, and occasional fitful revivals.

Meanwhile, on that first August morning, Crider steered me to the Personnel Department for the usual check-in formalities. I must have done the paperwork, but I don't even remember the look of the place. What I do remember, although not from that Monday, is taking the almost legendary "Morgue Course," a test for all beginning researchers. It was three sheets of questions which could be answered by delving into the magazine's voluminous reference library. In those days before the computer, the Morgue files consisted heavily of fat manila envelopes stuffed with untidy clippings and copies of research correspondence filed over the years. Some of the questions were straightforward; others were fairly tricky, designed to entrap the careless searcher. It took me most of the day to sift my way through to the answers. I never heard of anyone failing the Morgue Course. The point was not to pass or fail but to have an intense learning experience amid the zillions of facts in the editorial library. I was exhausted when I turned in my papers with the answers. I never heard back from it and have no idea whether I got an A or a C.

Life had two trainee jobs. One was in what was called "the cooler," a small office adjoining the Layout Room. The trainee was essentially a messenger, picking up pictures from archives elsewhere in Manhattan, carting layouts and photostats around the offices. It was a favored job because it involved hanging around with the sometimes rowdy and irreverent artists who inhabited the Layout Room. The other job, the one I received, was far more sedate. It was in the Picture Bureau. The trainee's principal occupation was visiting every office at the magazine every Monday morning, lugging a large square wire basket, and filling it with each editor's rejected photographs from the previous week. There were hundreds. I lugged the basket back to my desk in the Picture Bureau and began the chore of sorting them for return. Some went to *Life's* picture files; some to photo agencies or archives.

By accident or by intention, this job was a terrific introduction not only to the workings of the magazine but also to photography generally. My previous experience with photography had been with the small glossy snapshots from the neighborhood drugstore. Now there were stacks of riveting and gorgeous 11″ x 14″ enlargements and occasionally even larger photographs, each so exciting I used to wonder why they were in the reject basket. After a while, I could begin to see that, while they were all stunning, some were more stunning than others, as the editors saw quickly enough. Although an invaluable education just by itself, my Monday travels also taught me the location of the various departments. The top editors and the staff who oversaw foreign and domestic coverage were all on the 31st floor, along with the writers who wrote those stories and whose ranks I aspired to join. The so-called back-of-the-book departments were all downstairs on the 30th floor. These included such specialized coverages as religion, education, and nature. There was a lively entertainment department, where I was delighted to linger because of the marvelous photographs and portraits that lay around. The department was headed by a slender, fey gentleman named Tom Prideaux, who hailed from Michigan, and who, like many Midwesterners, quickly became the very model of Gotham cosmopolitanism. His assistant, Mary Logan Leatherbee, the sister of director Joshua Logan, was a beautiful, feisty woman, who seemed at first glance a dilettante, but who turned out to have spent some of World War II ferrying bombers to England and had hated flying ever since. There was also a large Science Department because *Life's* essays on atomic physics, childbirth, and psychiatry were some of the magazine's most honored achievements.

John Dille, who wrote about military affairs, had the desk next to mine. John once brought his pet boa constrictor to the office for a couple of days. Since I paled at the sight of a garter snake, I viewed John's boa—the largest live snake I'd ever seen—with something approaching panic. But John kept it in a drawer, where it snoozed quietly, or under an overturned wire basket if he had to be away from his desk. And at least he didn't ask me to pet it or hold it, which some of the more daring staffers were more than happy to do.

In the Picture Bureau I was the only male in a company of women. My boss was Dorothy Hoover, the head of the Picture Bureau, and my colleagues were the delightful women who worked for her, Ruth Lester, Natalie Kosek, Peggy Goldsmith, Mary Carr, Jane Bartels, Betty Doyle, and Maudie Milar. I was twenty-two and, even with the remnant of an upstate summer tan, I looked even younger than that. It sometimes felt as if I had a half dozen or more honorary aunts.

I began my Manhattan life in a windowless room above a Puerto Rican bar, across the street from Madison Square Garden. One day, there was an unusual throng around the Garden and I asked a cop what was happening. "Agh, it's Henry Wallace and his Commies havin' a meeting," he said. It was the Progressive Party Convention of 1948.

I next found a room that had a window, at least, uptown at Broadway and 110th Street, in a grand old building whose spacious, high-ceilinged apartments had been chopped and partitioned into warrens for graduate students at Columbia. In September, I begged a couple of extra days from Dorothy Hoover and went back to Hammondsport, where Peg and I were married. Afterward we entrained to Asbury Park for an abbreviated honeymoon. I still have a snapshot of us cavorting in bathing suits but freezing cold. I looked on the scrawny side of skinny, weighing then about 130 pounds, a weight I would never see again, thanks to Peggy's cooking and the glory of New York restaurants. I installed Peg in our new digs and we both

WEDDING DAY: *In 1948, gorgeous Peg and thin Charles in a brand-new suit from Richman Brothers in Elmira (thirty dollars, with a spare pair of pants) stood on the steps of St. Gabriel's, newly married and blissfully unaware of all that lay ahead.*

went to work, I at *Life* and she at Winthrop-Stearns, a downtown pharmaceutical firm where she proofread medicine labels and did other editorial chores. It was just as well we were very young, very much in love, and (mostly) indifferent to having to share a bathroom with four other apartments and a kitchen with twice that many. Our share of the refrigerator would hold two quarts of milk or the equivalent. We ate out when we could.

One early November night, after we'd been to a screening of Olivier's *Henry V,* we walked through Rockefeller Plaza, where we watched televison's first crude coverage of a presidential election on a huge screen in front of the RCA building. Some Time-Life people were helping the NBC team with the coverage. In a far cry from the election coverages that were to come, there were few graphics and many shots of men in shirtsleeves rushing about looking confused. But it was live, immediate, and engrossing. I probably wasn't perceptive enough to see that it was the wave of the future that would engulf *Life* and affect all of our lives.

After a while, I began to remember Jim Crider's remark about the writer who hadn't had a raise in months but didn't get the message. I wasn't expecting a raise, but I began to worry that my long tenure in the Picture Bureau—it had lasted at least six months—was intended to tell me something. My sorting didn't quite measure up? What else?

I think I did set a longevity record, but I was sprung at last, transferred to the section called "Newsfront," which oversaw the magazine's domestic news coverage. My successor in the Picture Bureau was Loudon Wainwright, a nephew of General Jonathan (Skinny) Wainwright, who'd survived the infamous Bataan Death March. Loudon had already published a short story in the *New Yorker* called "The Gentle Bounce." It made him the envy of the other writers. He would later write the best biography of *Life, The Great American Magazine,* published by Knopf in 1986.

Newsfront was presided over by a sturdy, tough-minded woman named Irene Saint, who ran a tight ship. Her coed staff varied from a neophyte like me to an experienced newspaper reporter like Dora Jane (Dodie) Hamblin, who'd worked for the Cedar Rapids *Gazette* and been a Red Cross staffer in Italy during the war.

With the passage of years, when you've scrambled your way up a few rungs up the ladder, it's possible for friendly acquaintances to assume that it's all been honey and jam and that the climb had always had a nice inevitability about it. But it ain't necessarily so, and probably never is. I spent most of my first year at *Life* scared to death behind a cheerful exterior, certain that I'd gotten in over my head and would likely be found out and sent packing at any moment. (I realize I'd felt the same way my first term or two at Harvard. I felt the same way in the Army, too, except that I was in no danger there of being sent packing.)

Especially after I escaped from the Picture Bureau and became a researcher in Newsfront, I lived with such angst it's a wonder I didn't grow an ulcer. The great Time-Life checking system called for the researcher to put a black dot over every word checked in the writer's basic text, and a red dot over every proper name checked, whether person or place. The old researchers' tale was three errors and you were out.

One of my first chores was to check the caption on a Picture of the Week of starlet Cleo Moore in a furry bikini making a snowball during a rare Los Angeles snowstorm. The writer, Bob Wallace (one of the magazine's best), had said it was so cold the oranges froze and dropped from the trees. I suspect Bob may have invented this as a perfectly plausible turn of events. I just couldn't find a source that confirmed it. (The researcher lived by sources he could cite.) The Morgue was no help and, late on a Saturday, I couldn't think of anybody to call. I walked the corridors debating what the devil to do. At last, I put black dots over the dreaded words and prepared to meet my doom the next week. Nothing came of it, of course; I assumed the oranges *did* fall off the trees.

A few weeks later, the national editor, Sid James, handed me a photostat of a Missouri River map and asked me to compile the data on the dam system on the river. My impression was that I was supposed to put the data on the map itself. I didn't have a clue as to how to begin. The Morgue came up with some data, and I just stared at the map for quite a while. Irene, my boss, discovered my plight and was furious that I'd been asked to do something that was really not my function and certainly beyond my competence. The cup passed from my lips, and the experience changed my luck, if not my life.

Almost the next day, memory says, Irene took me to lunch at Del Pezzo's, a second-floor Italian restaurant around the corner on 47th Street, a favorite spot for *Life* staffers. We had two and possibly three martinis, a not uncommon lunch potion in those days. (I'm not sure how we ever got any afternoon work done; today, after one martini at lunch, I'm desperately in need of a nap.) But Irene was on a double mission: one, to make sure I was on her team, which is to say, her side in her undeclared rivalry with her boss, Sid James; and, two, to pep me up by convincing me what a good and promising writer I was. My writing then consisted mostly of sending teletypes to the bureaus requesting pictures and information. She urged me to stand my ground and make my opinions known. I'm sure that it was the lunch that saved my job and my prospects. I had worries from time to time, but I was freed of the dark feeling that I'd be found out and sent back to Oswego County in failure and disgrace.

Irene, I learned years later, was known among researchers for her martini-fueled recruitment-to-her-side-and-pep-talk sessions. One of my writing contemporaries, William Brinkley, used such an incident in a novel, though I suspect it didn't happen to him; he was simply relating the legend.

In Newsfront, we mostly assigned stories to the bureaus and

stringers outside New York and, more important, took over the material when it arrived. We "sound-tracked" the photographs: learned the content and, having carried them to layout sessions in the managing editor's office, tried to describe each of the pictures as the editor flipped through them at high speeds. I suspect that the tense atmosphere was quite like film writers pitching story ideas to a studio executive. The managing editor during most of my days at *Life* in New York was Edward K. Thompson, who was by general agreement one of the true geniuses of photojournalism. Ed had come to *Life* from the *Milwaukee Journal,* which became famous for its photographic staff and its use of pictures. He was legendary for his skills at putting picture stories together, and also for his way of expressing his wishes in a series of often indecipherable mumbles and grunts emerging past a well-chewed cigar. Frequently after a session in his office, the art editors and the news editors would cluster outside and ask each other, "What did he say?" No one quite dared go back in and ask him what he *had* said, and the pages were dummied with fingers crossed.

Thompson's taste was unerring. One day, the foreign news staff brought in a stack of photographs of still-devastated Berlin. One of the writers said, "Oh, God, more ruins." Ed glanced at him dismissively and returned to the pictures. It was an essay by Walter Sanders on his return to his native Berlin for the first time since before the war. It included a dramatic photograph of his old landlady, evidently an anti-Semite, staring down at him from the top of the stairs with a look of icy contempt. Ed had spotted it, and indeed saw the power of Sanders's whole essay. Ruins, indeed.

Thompson gave the magazine its turn-the-page excitement from front to back. He made decisions with amazing swiftness and was usually right the first time, although he cheerfully changed his mind when, confronted with the pasteups, he thought of a better layout. Late on a Saturday night, when *Life* went to press in Chicago, Ed's decisions to revamp a story would occasionally bring groans of fatigue, but I think there was usually agreement that those decisions made things better.

One Saturday night, after a late shake-up in the layouts, Natalie Kosek, one of the Picture Bureau women, while rushing about with some new prints, said philosophically, "Every damn week we pretend we've never put out a magazine before."

Some Saturday night closings were later than others. One memorable Saturday, I walked into the Time-Life building at ten o'clock and didn't walk out again until nine the next morning. That Saturday, the president's daughter, Margaret Truman, married Clifton Daniel in Independence, Missouri, and the film hadn't arrived and been processed until late at night, when the layout and writing and editing could finally begin. By Monday morning, as on all Monday mornings, the so-called make-ready copies were on editors' desks. By midweek, some seven million copies of the issue had been distributed. It was a remarkable technological feat. I sometimes wondered how many readers appreciated what an achievement it really was.

I went through a baptism of fire as an out-of-the-office reporter and I suppose as an out-of-my-depth neophyte. Jim Bell of *Time*, in "The New Army" series, had reported that unscrupulous landlords near Fort Dix, New Jersey, were gouging young married GIs living off the base. Irene assigned me and the photographer Lisa Larsen to go over to Wrightstown and document the story. We got a memorable photograph of a young couple living in what had been a "chicken coop," lit by one bare bulb. But we were also chased off another property by a landlord with a shotgun, and were threatened with lawsuits by other landlords, charging invasion of privacy. One angry woman also threatened to lay the matter before Boake Carter, the Paul Harvey of his day, and to take us to court as well. Doors were slammed in our faces, and I suddenly became aware that it was one thing to write about a situation and quite another to photograph it.

The threat of lawsuits scared me, and I reported it to Irene. She set up a meeting with Jack Dowd, a tall, unflappable Irishman who was *Life*'s in-house counsel. Jack said, approximately, "The woman can't sue us in New Jersey; we don't do business there. We'll send thirty photographers over to her place and take pictures of every piece of chicken shit in sight. Then we'll get her in front of a New Deal judge here in New York and she'll be lucky if *she* doesn't go to jail herself." It was a wonderful overstatement, but a blessed relief to hear. After the story ran, there wasn't a peep from the woman or any of the other landlords.

What I remember most from the last months of that first year at *Life* in New York was that Peg and I were sprung from our one room in that warren on West 110th Street. The postwar housing shortage was still severe in 1949. The imaginative real estate mogul William Zeckendorf had persuaded Time, Inc., to lease a whole apartment building at York Avenue and 91st Street so it could then sublease the units to its employees. We'd put our names on the waiting list and our turn finally came.

Our apartment was essentially one room, with bedroom and living room combined, but with separate kitchen and bath and all virtually brand new. The foreign news editor of *Life* and several others we knew or recognized lived in the same building. We were all young, and, as it turned out, fertile—so much so that the place went down in history as the *"Time* Incubator." Peg became pregnant for the first time, but miscarried. This saddened us. That Peg might not be able to carry a child to term also worried and depressed us, who both wanted children. But a few months later, Peg was pregnant again and, I'm happy to report, safely gave birth to Chuck Junior.

My years with *Life* and then *Time* present themselves now as a series of surprises, most of them pleasant and all of them rewarding.

By midsummer 1949, I'd been with *Life* as trainee and green reporter for a year. I hadn't yet done any of the writing for publication for which Jim Crider had presumably recruited me, none of those small captions that Carvel Collins had mentioned so mockingly. The only evidence that I might be a writer had come a few months earlier, when I saw an item in Walter Winchell's column about an eccentric rich old codger who flew expensive model airplanes from the roof of his building on Wall Street, to the amusement of passers-by. This didn't strike me especially as a piece for *Life;* I thought of it more as a "Notes and Comments" piece for the *New Yorker.* But, one noontime, I took the subway down to Wall Street and made some inquiries. No one had ever seen any model airplanes or heard of the old codger. The item may well have been the invention of some press agent trying to ingratiate himself with Walter. I went back to the office and wrote the story up in what I thought of as the style of the *New Yorker* and showed it to Irene for her amusement. She sent it along to the managing editor, Joe Thorndike, who was about to leave to start *American Heritage* magazine. Thorndike scrawled a congratulatory note on the column and sent it back to Irene. That was the beginning and end of the story, but it did my heart a power of good. Later in the summer, Irene announced that she'd decided to send me to *Life*'s Chicago bureau as a correspondent.

In its way, this was at least as significant an event as having been sprung from the Picture Bureau. It would also be an opportunity to acquire some much-needed journalistic experience.

Toddling Town

M ort Sahl once remarked that Chicago was the only city he knew where an only child could play cops and robbers. In the summer of 1949, Chicago still seemed very much the city that had been celebrated by Carl Sandburg, *The Front Page, The Untouchables,* and Nelson Algren's *A Walk On the Wild Side.* It had a wondrous windy vitality and the feeling of a wide open town, flavored by the ghost of Al Capone. Clark Street, where John Dillinger was shot leaving a cinema with the Lady in Red, was lined with strip joints where your wallet, if not your life, was at risk.

The office had booked Peggy and me into the Wellington Arms, a residential hotel overlooking Lake Michigan. Most bureau people used the hotel until they found permanent digs. We spent a few merry weeks there and then found an apartment only a few blocks from the hotel on the Near North Side. In late October, I took Peg by cab to Ravenswood Hospital, where our first child and son, Chuck Junior, was born.

The Time-Life bureau was then at 230 North Michigan Avenue, not far from the Chicago River. On my first day at work, eager to make a good impression, I'd found a barber shop that opened early and had my ears lifted and my hair drenched with Brilliantine, which made me look like a recent arrival from a farm in central Iowa. I got to the office at nine o'clock to find secretary Millie Lytle at her desk, thoroughly bemused. It turned out nobody got in before ten. But I'd been assigned a desk and I sat down with a paper to wait for my new colleagues to arrive.

It was a remarkable office. The bureau chief was a wonderful character named Hugh Moffett, who later, as the domestic news editor of *Life* in New York, would inspire a whole generation of *Life* reporters and writers.

Just after ten that first morning, as the correspondents began to arrive, I was surprised and delighted to see Bill Glasgow. We'd met and talked at a journalism conference two or three years before. He was then just completing a year as a Nieman Fellow at Harvard. He had worked as the labor reporter for the *Chicago Sun-Times,* and now he had the same beat for *Time.* Bill introduced us to the innovative and much-studied planned community of Park Forest, built on the former golf course just south of Chicago, where Bill and the other pioneer settlers were sometimes ankle-deep in mud until certain drainage problems were solved. Peggy and I and Chuck Junior, then about a year old, moved to Park Forest; our second child, Katy, was born a few months after we'd settled in there. Near the end of his career, Bill would go off to Venice, Italy, where he'd live in a flat above a *taverna* and occasionally commute to London to do broadcasts for BBC Radio.

One of my new associates on the *Life* side, whom I'd known briefly in New York, was Norman Ross, a large, handsome fellow with a widow's peak in the style of the film star Robert Taylor, which women seemed to find enviable. Norm, who had a bewitching naïveté for a man in his thirties, became the star of one of the legends of the Wellington Arms, where he had a corner apartment. One lovely, breezy morning, he arose, opened his windows, took a shower, and, for some fortunate reason, put his pajamas back on. When he went back into the living room, a stiff breeze off Lake Michigan was blowing his books and papers about and the door to

JOURNALIST AT THE TYPEWRITER: *Self-romanticizing as a hard-bitten rewrite man, with hat tilted back and pipe in mouth, I was the very model of an insouciant journalist unfazed by deadlines. Photo by Peggy Champlin.*

the corridor, which he'd left on the chain for better ventilation, was flapping free, the wind having snapped the chain. Norm fought his way across the room and seized the door. Then the wind suddenly changed and he found himself in the corridor with the door locked behind him. Just across the hall from Norm lived a pretty vocalist who appeared on a local television show. When he knocked and the singer started to open the door, he said, "Don't open it. I'm Mr. Ross, your neighbor across the hall, and I'm locked out, but it's very simple. If you will just call the desk and ask them to send up a bellman with a passkey that will solve everything." There was a pause and the singer said with a giggle, "Mr. Ross, I will be glad to call the desk and have them send up a bellman with a passkey. I just think you should know that they won't believe either one of us."

Another of the *Time* reporters in the bureau was Jim Conant, the son of the former president of Harvard. Jim was a liberal activist who campaigned to stop the Chicago newspapers' policy of race labeling, for example, identifying black miscreants as Negroes. He'd been in the submarine service during World War II, and it had left him with a kind of impatient disregard for the insignificant matters that sometimes interested *Time*'s editors. Jim wasn't happy with *Time* and, as can happen, it became mutual. His father wrote to Luce to find out why this was so. In his reply to President Conant, Luce said essentially that Jim's putts and irons were satisfactory, but that his drives were disappointing. Jim went to work for the International Paper Company.

Another member of the *Time* staff was Lew Spence, who was elegant, bordering on aristocratic, and sometimes seemed more British than American. He was a Harvard graduate, Class of 1941 or thereabouts. In winter, he wore a black, ankle-length great coat with a brown fur collar that you sensed had belonged to a grandfather who took good care of his clothes. Lou was an awfully good reporter and an even better writer. But, like Jim Conant, he wasn't made for the long haul at *Time* and left to become a communications consultant, teaching writing to executive recruiters.

The Chicago bureau was the beginning of my close acquaintance with that special breed of man, the *Life* photographer. The most endearing of the breed was Wallace Kirkland, who later became the first *Life* photographer to reach retirement age—only because he was well into middle age when he was first hired. Kirk had been born on a plantation in Jamaica, which was leveled by a hurricane, destroying the family fortune in the process. He made his way to Chicago, where he lived and worked at Jane Addams's Hull House, a pioneering charity settlement. Addams herself recruited Kirkland to take photographs for the benefit of Hull House. Soon enough, his dedication and skill with the camera brought him to the attention of *Life*. He worked largely in and around Chicago, but made one memorable trip to India, where he photographed Gandhi and Nehru. He loved nature photography. He took pictures of prairie dogs, rarely seen in the flesh, then or now. He set up an experiment in his basement in Oak Park and, after weeks of trying, got an amazing sequence of photos of a dragonfly emerging from its cocoon. Kirk was also a Rabelaisian figure, whose photos of beautiful nudes never made it into a magazine but enlivened the scenery on the bulletin boards in the office.

Ralph Crane, a tall, almost spectrally thin Swiss, was another of the Chicago photographers. One day, there was a race riot in suburban Cicero, Illinois, and we all rushed out to cover it. A black fireman and his wife had moved into an apartment in the, until then, all-white suburb. A crowd of locals had begun throwing rocks at the brick apartment building. By the time a team of us from the bureau got to the scene, the fireman and his wife had somehow escaped and fled, and some ten thousand people were throwing rocks at the building, which now looked like it had been bombed. Eventually a National Guard company arrived and held the crowd in check.

Crane had just acquired one of the new ultralight titanium step lad-
ders. He climbed the ladder to take pictures of the crowd. But when
someone threw a rock, narrowly missing him, he clambered down,
folded up the ladder, and left it beside a lamppost. After dark, the
crowd, most of whom presumably had to get up and go to work in
the morning, began to disperse and we were heading for our cars
when Ralph discovered that somebody had stolen his stepladder. He
was angry and aghast. "How could somebody do that?" he asked,
after ten thousand people had assaulted an empty building.

My three years in Chicago provided another part of my postgraduate education as a journalist. I helped to cover political cam-
paigns; a refinery strike; a steel strike; the Korean War as it affected
the small city of Columbus, Indiana; a traditional high school basketball game; an extraordinary apartment building on the black
South Side called "The Mecca"; floods along the Missouri—an
amazing segment of the spectrum of *Life*. I was to find years later that
all those experiences became invaluable resources when I began reviewing films: in a surprising number of cases, the films reflected or
tried to reflect one segment or another of real life.

Chicago was then, and I suspect still is, one of the liveliest political scenes in the country. I hadn't been there long when a legendary
old alderman named Hinky-Dink Kenna (pronounced "keNAW")
was gathered to his Maker. *Life* went to cover the funeral, expecting a
massive turnout, mounds of flowers, and at least one huge floral
horseshoe with "Good-bye, Hinky-Dink" inscribed on a banner. The
Life bureau chief, Frank Campion, thought there might be ten thousand on hand for the Mass. There were indeed hundreds of dollars
worth of floral tributes, although I don't remember whether they included a horseshoe. The church was full, but the crowd didn't spill
out onto the street. Frank went up to a lesser pol and one of Hinky-
Dink's heirs and asked why there wasn't a more significant turnout.

"I tell you what it is," the pol said. "Hinky-Dink was never much of a one for going to funerals, and if you want people to come to your funeral, you gotta go to theirs."

The principal political figure as I arrived was Mayor Ed Kelly, "Big Ed," as he was known on the street. After he left office, Kelly maintained a headquarters in the Merchandise Mart behind a door marked "Engineer." When Big Ed died, *Life* once again anticipated a large turnout. The church was in fact packed and there was a small overflow at the door. Yet this was Big Ed Kelly, who'd done so much to ensure the nomination of FDR during the Democratic Convention of 1932 by having the cry of "We want Roosevelt" echo throughout the Chicago Stadium like a message from God. The bureau chief once again sought out a wise operative in city politics, asking why there weren't even more people at the funeral. "Well," the pol said, "it's not as if Mrs. Kelly had died and Big Ed was still alive."

The pols and the politics were all fascinating. The political atmosphere was somehow so intimate there was never that sense of learning what was happening from newspapers with distant datelines. It was all happening where you were.

I still remember the November night in 1950 when Senator Scott Lucas was defeated by a little-known upstart from Pekin, Illinois, named Everett McKinley Dirksen. Lucas, who, until that night, had been the Democratic Majority Leader in the Senate, wasn't so much philosophical as furious about his defeat. Toward midnight, he appeared before a battery of microphones and cameras in the Democratic headquarters in the Blackstone Hotel. Lucas strode to the microphone and snapped, "Boys, get this the first time. I'm not going to repeat it." He made his concession to Dirksen and strode out of the room into forgetful history.

Two of the most ambitious stories I worked on in Chicago never saw the light of print. That was always one of the penalties of working for *Life* and, later on, for *Time*. The difference was that at *Time* I was working in my own element—words. The stories for *Life* involved photography, pictures, arrangements, patience. My most pleasant experience was working on a picture essay on Edgar Lee Masters's *Spoon River Anthology*, whose poems had the dead speak from the grave about their lives, marked and inspired by their tombstones. Often the tombstones actually existed in the cemeteries in the Abraham Lincoln country around New Salem and Petersburg, Illinois. A fine photographer named Myron Davis and I spent several days in that beautiful, peaceful countryside. We photographed tombstones, the carved angels, and all the emblems of lives remembered, but probably now forgotten. We photographed a wonderful old man, ninety-two, named Harvey Rutledge, who was a second cousin of the Anne Rutledge beloved of Lincoln. Naturally Harvey, even at his ripe age, was too young to have known his cousin, but she was kin. We photographed him shooting pool. It was a lovely picture. He had what I think of as a Norman Rockwell face.

We were shooting a black-and-white essay at a time when color pictures were getting more and more numerous in the magazine. I suspect we were just a little too late, as beautiful as the pictures were. They were worth an exhibit in any gallery, but I'm not aware that they ever had one. Not least among his virtues, every *Life* photographer had to have a gift for philosophical resignation.

I did a long photo essay on the University of Illinois with another photographer, Wayne Miller, who worked as an assistant to Edward Steichen on the historic "Family of Man" exhibition at the Museum of Modern Art. The essay was to be one of a series in the magazine on various kinds of higher education—the small liberal arts colleges, the private universities, the big land grant universities like Illinois. We photographed everything at Champaign-Urbana—the president, the deans, the resident string quartet, fraternities, sororities, classrooms, seminars, counseling sessions, sports. The stack of prints grew to more than a foot high. Going well beyond dutiful matters of record, some of the photos were very lively and even sexy. But when the education writer who had assigned the story presented the stack to the managing editor, he dismissed the pictures without even looking at them. His summary judgment, according to the writer assigned the story, was "We've done enough about higher education." I wasn't a highly paid worker, but Miller, a fine freelance photographer, certainly was. What the bill for that assignment was I can't even guess, but *Life's* philosophy always was that the more material you can cast aside, the better your final product will be. You could certainly have filled a second magazine with material *Life* discarded, and it would have been a damn good magazine.

The main reason for sending me to the Chicago bureau was to give me much-needed experience doing stories. A second, slightly subtler reason was to meld my naïve and often sentimental optimism with an invigorating dose of skepticism. It seemed to me that my three years in Chicago succeeded admirably on both counts. I sometimes felt awash in reportorial experience. As for my naïveté, I hadn't lost all of it, of course, but I was learning to be sharp-eyed and doubtful about story suggestions from publicists, even suave and likable ones. But neither then nor later did I see myself as a hard-hitting investigative reporter who knew how to dig out the guilty secrets buried in the files of a county courthouse.

One of the Chicago aldermen I got to know was Robert Merriam, the son of a distinguished historian at the University of Chicago and the author of a fine account of the Battle of the Bulge, *Dark December.* Bob Merriam was impeccably honest. I remember once asking him how he got along with some of his fellow aldermen, whose reputations were, to say the least, cloudy. "Ah, well," Merriam said. "I've just enough larceny in my own heart to be able to guess what the other guys are up to."

I'm not sure it was larceny I found in my own heart, but I began to feel that I'd added a certain amount of savvy, which replaced the gullibility that used to be there.

Moff

PORTRAIT OF A COUNTRY SLICKER

In the very beginning, the prevailing atmosphere of Time, Inc., was heavily Ivy League. The cofounders, Henry Luce and Briton Hadden, had been together at the exclusive preparatory school Hotchkiss and at Yale, where they'd first conceived the publication that would become *Time*. Their first important executive hiring was also an Ivy Leaguer: Roy Larsen, Harvard '21, who served as ad and circulation manager of the new magazine.

Some of the early writers and editors were also recruited from Eastern schools. Later it began to be felt that the magazines's orientation was too Eastern. At one point, Luce moved the headquarters of Time, Inc., to Cleveland briefly, that the magazine might better reflect what was going on in the Heartland. It was a bit like a Bostonian announcing he was going to drive to California by way of Worcester. The magazine's headquarters returned to New York soon enough.

Yet, more and more, *Time* and the later magazines began to be staffed by non-Eastern types, bringing to *Time* high reputations established in Des Moines, St. Louis, New Orleans, Omaha, and even California. These writers and editors, most notably Edward K. Thompson, later to be the longtime managing editor of *Life*, gave the magazines a quite genuinely natural national outlook. Several of the top editors at *Time* magazine from the 1930s onward came from the *St.*

Louis Post-Dispatch and the *St. Louis Globe Democrat.* One of the most delightful and talented men I ever worked for was Hugh Oliver Moffett, a native of Galena, Illinois, which also gave the world Ulysses S. Grant. Moffett had worked for the Cedar Rapids *Gazette.* One of his editorial colleagues once remarked that Moff was the original "country slicker," which is to say, he did his best to conceal a penetrating and cosmopolitan intelligence under a thin and transparent veneer of down-home mannerisms. He walked with a kind of forward-leaning gait, like a man who'd plowed many a furrow in his youth. This was probably as misleading as his folksy mannerisms.

When I first met him, Moffett was running the Chicago bureau. What he did on the way from Galena to Cedar Rapids to Chicago I don't know. Moff wasn't a man who talked about himself much. Like many journalists who ended up at *Time* and *Life,* it's a reasonable guess he'd been a stringer who'd caught the attention of the editors by his energy, imagination, and story sense. He was the more effective administrator by never seeming to administer, creating the illusion that things took care of themselves while shaping the stories that emerged from his bureau with the subtlest of hints. After a hitch covering the Korean War, based in Tokyo and commuting to the battle zones, he went to New York as the national affairs editor of *Life.* By then, I was in New York writing for him and being exposed to his sometimes sardonic humor.

One Saturday night in Chicago, during a lull in the process of putting *Life* to bed, when Moffett and some of the staff were sitting around, one of the young reporters suggested a story for the magazine. Moffett heard him out and then said, "What you have to remember is that there are two kinds of magazines. There is the 'Gee whiz' magazine and there is the 'Ah, shit' magazine. *Life* is a 'Gee whiz' magazine and never forget it."

Moffett wasn't quite as cynical as that suggests, but he knew very well what the magazine wanted and didn't want. And *Life* wasn't quite the "Gee whiz" magazine he'd made it out to be. It didn't shy away from stories that revealed the country and the world in their least attractive moments. What was not part of the *Life* philosophy was cynicism. In its charter, Henry Luce had defined the mission of *Life* back in 1936; the key phrase was "to see life and see it whole." Moffett had no quarrel with what Luce said, but felt you needed to be a little skeptical in thinking about any story.

Moffett had a boisterous laugh, revealing an unexpected gold tooth. He was fond of a raucous ballad called "The Hermit of Sharktooth Shoal," a parody of the ballads of Robert W. Service. After a while, many of us could shout the first few lines in unison. The parody was written in the late 1920s by a screenwriter named Edward Paramore, Jr. It begins:

> The North Countree is a hard country
> That mothers a bloody brood.
> Her icy arms hold hidden charms
> For the greedy, the sinful and lewd.

When things got slow on Saturday night, Moffett would also lead the troops in singing "It Was Sad When the Great Ship Went Down." I think that, among *Life*'s editors, there was no one else who combined so high a degree of professional competence with such joie de vivre.

Once, in our Chicago period, Moffett went off to Des Moines to cover the annual convention of the militant National Farmers' Union and asked me to come along to help with the reporting. The man who could sing "It Was Sad When the Great Ship Went Down" late in the evening was also the man who could report cogently on agricultural price support policies, the difference between a gilt and a barrow, and the price from day to day of cows and other livestock items delivered to the Chicago stockyards. Moffett was covering the convention because of the hot issues that would be raised there, mostly involving parity and other farm questions controversial at that moment. I confess I found all these matters as obscure as Jesuit philosophy. But Moffett gave me a particular angle to follow and I was able to do a quick study. We were sitting side by side in the press room of the convention center working on manual typewriters, which were then par for the course. I wasn't actually writing yet, but awaiting signs from above. Hammering away on his copy, Moffett came to the end of a paragraph and said, "Here's where your stuff goes." He got out of his chair and invited me to sit and add my words. I don't think I can remember a moment when I felt more intimidated and more out of my depth. Ransacking my notes and my understanding, I read Moffett's previous two or three paragraphs and somehow batted out a paragraph of my own. I moved back to my own seat, and Moffett resumed his; to my great relief, he nodded approvingly at what I'd said and went on with the rest of his file.

Back in the Chicago bureau a few days later, Moffett called me into his big corner office, holding a piece of paper in his hand. It was my expense account. He said, "You indicated on Friday that you spent twenty cents for bus fare." I remembered that indeed I had taken a bus to the convention center.

"Are you trying to make the rest of us look corrupt?" he asked. "Friday night after the session we were sitting in the bar and I know that you bought a round of drinks for the table. That was a legitimate expense. Why isn't it in your report?"

He handed the expense report back to me and said, "You'd better go over it again. It's inaccurate and incomplete . . . and we never, ever take buses."

That was a perfect example of why all his reporters, myself most especially included, loved Hugh Moffett. It wasn't that our expense accounts thereafter were in any degree larcenous. It was just that they were more accurate and the legendary lady in New York who oversaw our expense accounts, the improbably named Minnie Magazine, never, I think, had cause to complain of our honesty and integrity. Or if she did, she never let on.

Once an Illinois Central train derailed in mid-state, with many injuries and some loss of life. While we were making phone calls as fast as we could to put someone on a chartered plane to photograph the carnage, one of our staff photographers wandered back to the office from a trip. When he asked about all the excitement and was told, he said, "Oh, yeah, I flew over it and I saw some stuff on the ground." Moffett said nothing at the time, but the next day, he posted a memo on the bulletin board, saying that, in the event of the Second Coming of Christ, staffers were to start coverage immediately and not wait for an assignment from either the bureau or New York.

Though undoubtedly a skeptic and often a cynic, Moffett was first and always a newsman. He never lost the thrill of sending us out to cover a major news event like the train wreck. After his days as the Chicago bureau chief, he went off to cover the Korean War. He returned to serve as the domestic news editor of *Life* and eventually retired to Vermont, where he won election to the state legislature, one of the few Democrats in sight. Of the dozens of us who worked for and with Hugh Moffett over the years, I think there was no one who didn't become a better, more skeptical, more dedicated reporter and writer because of the association.

Interlude at 5,280 Feet

My small-*l* life at the start of the 1950s was in the hands of Irene Saint, head of the domestic news bureau and chief of correspondents, and Ed Thompson, managing editor, at Time-Life's headquarters in New York. After my three years in Chicago, Irene said that Ed wanted me to come back to New York and write. That was, after all, what I'd been hired to do. But, having tasted the joys of life in the field doing stories, keeping crazy, long hours, and experiencing the world as it is, going back to a desk and writing was not what I wanted to do, at least not for a while. I asked Irene to let me stay in a bureau if she possibly could. She called me back and said, fairly grimly, that she didn't think it was good for my career to turn down the invitation to write in New York, but that Thompson had agreed (with exasperation, she hinted) that I could stay in the field a while more. She was sending me to Denver to work with Edmond Burr Ogle, the bureau chief there, a sturdy, balding, cheerful journalist who'd been a stringer in New Orleans. The special assignment of going to the small, two-man bureau was that I'd be reporting for both *Time* and *Life*, depending on how the workload went. (Electing to stay in the field longer did not affect my career in any degree, but it did cause me some uneasy nights.)

We were now four of us, a son, Chuck Junior, and a daughter, Katy. We were expecting, too, a third child who turned out to be a

148

son named John. We drove to Denver in our newly bought four-door Plymouth sedan, which turned out to be the least lovable car I'd ever owned. I stashed the family in a motel while I went to the bureau's small quarters in a downtown office building to meet Ogle, an office secretary, and a freelance photographer named Carl Iwasaki, a young Nisei who'd been interned with his family at Hart Mountain during the war years. Carl did all the bureau's picture work.

Denver was on the move. There was a uranium boom southwest of town and there was an oil boom in eastern Colorado—and the economic ripples of both were being felt in Denver itself. Then as now, Denver was a beautiful city, but one with a split personality. It was the cattle-raising center for all of Colorado to the east and south, but it was also the mercantile and major government center for the whole Rocky Mountain region. I once saw a Denver street scene that seemed to symbolize this two-in-one city perfectly. Waiting for the light to change, side by side but not together, were a man in a Brooks Brothers suit and a rancher in a ten-gallon hat, denim clothes, and cowboy boots. My amused guess was that the rancher was the one with all the money.

As usual, the first chore was to find a place to live. In no time at all, we located a little house on the east side of town on something called "Richthofen Parkway," named for the family of the World War I German ace. We bought the house for $13,750. It was our first. I planted two juniper bushes in the front yard, an unusual undertaking because the soil there, as in much of Denver, was covered by a layer of loess compacted to the approximate density of cast iron. I had to dig down an inch or two where I could, fill the hole with water, wait for it to soak in, dig down a few more inches, and repeat the process. Houses have been built in the time it took me to get those two bushes into the ground, but when I finally did, I felt like a real homeowner.

Denver in those days was a real boom town, with an electric vitality and the pervasive smell of money being made and spent with equal glee. The oil companies seemed to have hundreds of secretaries, each sexier than the last. Every late afternoon seemed to be party time at places like Shaner's Restaurant and at the bars in the Brown Palace and the other midtown hotels. The drinks flowed and the money flowed—it was as if, within that well-defined set, there was no tomorrow.

The town was filled with wildcatters, promoters who operated by getting hold of leases for what they hoped would be good drilling sites. They would then divide the wells (not yet drilled of course) into eighths. The wildcatters reserved one-eighth for themselves and one-eighth for the drillers and sold the remaining six-eighths, which were subdivided, sometimes into sixteenths and even thirty-seconds, to as many investors as they could recruit. Even if a well became what was called a "duster," or dry well, the wildcatter usually kept enough cash in hand to live another day.

When I'd been in Denver long enough to begin to get the feel of the territory, I read about a young wildcatter named Joe Hicks, who'd had the phenomenal luck of hitting nine producing wells in a row. Handsome, charming, and persuasive, Joe was from a small city in Georgia. "Lordy," he laughed, "how the money rolls in." But Joe was realistic about the possibility that his luck could change. He said, "I can buy champagne for everybody in a nightclub and still be better off than when I invest in a bad lease." Sure enough, Joe's streak of hits ended at nine in a row. Thereafter he couldn't find oil at a gas station. Late one night, he and I drove out into eastern Colorado in his Hudson Hornet to see a well in progress. They were drilling what they called the "core sand"; the cores were laid into troughs for microscopic examination by his geologist. It was midnight and the scene was garishly lit by a string of bare bulbs on temporary poles. As we watched, the geologist shook his head sadly and patted Joe on the shoulder. It was a duster as sure as God made sour green apples. Joe and I got back in the Hornet and sped off toward Denver. We hadn't gone far when we were pulled over by a state trooper. It just wasn't Joe's night. He got out and went to sit with the trooper in the patrol car. But when he came back, he was grinning. "No ticket," he said. My guess has always been that he told the sad story of his duster and the trooper elected not to increase his pain.

Because Joe's luck had changed for the worse and *Life* didn't like to celebrate bad news, our story never ran. Yet it seemed to me that when Joe had been on his winning streak, he symbolized the exuberance of all the wildcatters. I kept in touch with him for the rest of my time in Denver. Toward the end, he'd let me pay for our occasional lunches. I last saw him when I was writing in New York and Joe had come to town promoting a liquid shoe polish for shoes of all colors that you only had to apply, not brush. He left me a bottle. I tried it on a pair of my shoes and the leather cracked. I never saw Joe again. I only hope that some of the pleasure and occasional riches he'd brought to so many people returned to him like the bread cast upon the water.

The principal joy of working for *Life* was that so many of the stories were a pleasure to do. Whether they finally ran in the magazine or not, getting there was all the fun, sometimes amounting to a paid vacation, with scenery and even occasionally a sense of adventure.

One of the stories I did for *Time* involved a high school science teacher named Elmer Halseth from Rock Springs, Wyoming, who wrote to at least a dozen young but already well-known American artists asking for paintings for his high school. The walls of the school soon blazed with their beautiful work. Rock Springs was a railroad junction town, still wide open at the time, with brothels flourishing. The town needed all the art it could find. Elmer later became a state legislator.

Driving back to Denver, I took a two-lane highway that rose through the mountains until, at its highest point, the road seemed to drop away beneath me. On the valley below, I saw an ordinary car far off with a state trooper's patrol car just behind it. By the time I reached the valley floor, the ordinary car was gone but the patrol car was still there. The trooper flagged me down and said, "You're the only two cars I've seen so far today and wouldn't you know you'd come one right after the other."

That was the real thrill of working out of Denver. There were those endless vistas, the grandeur of the huge, dwarfing mountains, the feeling of isolation amid a land so thinly populated it was a little scary. But it was also magnificent.

The most thrilling assignment of those days began with a phone call from a researcher in New York. *Life* was producing "The World We Live In," a look at the globe in all its glory, for which the editors needed a series of illustrations of geological processes such as erosion and weathering. Because *Life* did nothing by halves, it had arranged with a geologist from the United States Geological Survey in Denver to let a *Life* photographer and reporter accompany him on a two-week trip to the Four Corners area of the Colorado Plateau, where Colorado, Arizona, New Mexico, and Utah touch. The geologist, Charlie Hunt, had years ago had the great privilege of mapping the geology of the area for the first time since the legendary Major John Wesley Powell had mapped the Colorado River itself in the 1860s. Now, with the uranium boom in full swing, Hunt was looking over the area for possible formations that might contain deposits of uranium ore.

I got the reporting assignment, for which I am forever grateful. The photographer turned out to be Andreas Feininger, the son of the famous German Expressionist painter, Lionel Feininger. Andreas was a sturdy, intense, bespectacled perfectionist who frequently shot technically demanding photographs. One of his most famous was of the skeleton of an anaconda coiled as if ready to squeeze anything in sight.

TOURING THE WEST FOR *LIFE*: *In 1953, I toured the Colorado Plateau country with geologist Charlie Hunt, his wife, Alice, and photographer Andreas Feininger, at left, leaning against the jeep.*

Charlie was to be accompanied by his beautiful wife, Alice, an anthropologist. We foregathered in Denver and headed west in a jeep loaded with four sleeping bags, tarpaulins, and blankets, an enormous pile of photographic gear, and a modest pile of provisions, including a case of Coors beer.

For the next two weeks, we crisscrossed the high country, often going far off such dirt tracks as there were and following formations. "Ah," Charlie Hunt would say, "there's the Windgate sandstone I was looking for." I've forgotten the names of all the varieties of rock and vast formations we stopped to examine at Uncompahgre Peak, on the Book Cliffs plateau, at the San Rafael Swell, and at the many other exotically named places we visited. But for one night at a motel, where we could take badly needed hot showers, we slept out under the stars in our sleeping bags. And, thanks to the cold, clear, mile-and-a-half-high air, we all slept like logs. That is, all of us except Feininger, who proved to have a genius for spreading his tarpaulin, sleeping bag, and blanket directly on top of spiky Russian thistle, and who insisted on sleeping fully clothed. As anyone who's used an old-fashioned sleeping bag and blanket learns, unlikely as it may seem, on a chilly night, unless you strip to your underwear, you're likely to overheat and end up with your blanket bunched at your feet and the rest of you shivering mightily. Now and then, throughout the night, we'd be awakened by low moans and Germanic curses as Andreas tried to shift off the thistle and somehow get warm.

Like many *Life* photographers, Feininger was an imperious taskmaster, commanding stops so that he could take pictures that struck him as suitably scenic. The editors had briefed Charlie by phone on the kinds of things they wanted. So, from time to time, he would explain with tactful caution when a proposed picture didn't really illustrate the point the editors had in mind.

One afternoon, we were driving through a narrow, shallow canyon with a roadbed hardly wider than the jeep and with rock walls on each side dozens of feet high. Charlie pointed out that this was one of those places in the desert where, if you saw a cloud ten miles away, you got out as fast as you could because even a brief shower would send a flash flood roaring through, sweeping everything before it. This day there were no clouds. Suddenly, around a small bend, we came upon a smaller canyon leading off to one side. Charlie parked the jeep and led us into a large cave that was, I suppose, thirty feet wide. In it were some benches and some metal lockers caked with rust. Alice gasped when she saw the place. What a wonderful moment it was for both of them. Years before, she'd come out from Boston to marry Charlie. She'd ridden in a pickup truck and her wedding dress to this very cavern, which, Charlie said, had been a ritual site for the Penitentes. There they were married by a priest who'd also driven out. Alice hadn't seen the place since the day they were married.

The state of Arizona rises from north to south, the rise ending suddenly in the east at the Mogollon Rim, a 100-mile-long band of cliffs that drop hundreds of feet to the beginning of a vast pine forest, the largest primeval pine forest in the country. Charlie, who had a wonderful sense of the dramatic, drove us to a clearing just off the Mogollon Rim Road, which ran along the very edge of the cliffs, and said we would camp there for the night. It was, of all the nights on our trip, the most memorable. We were surrounded by majestic pines, the night air was bracingly cold, the view to the south before the light faded was awesome, and I had that feeling, as I'd often had on the trip, that I'd never see this place again. Zane Grey had written novels about it, the most famous being *Under the Tonto Rim*. At the far end of the road, on the lower level, was the town of Show Low, Arizona, named after a poker game. We wended our way down from the rim and ultimately stopped on the south bank of the Colorado River, where I took off my shoes and socks and waded in, just to say I had. The water was brown with sand and moved with surprising force; indeed, you could hear rocks bumping along under the water. We were at El Vado de los Padres—the crossing of the Fathers— where Father Silvestre Escalante and his people had forded the river on one of their ancient explorations.

Back in Denver, I wrote pages of captions with crude sketches of the terrain to go with Feininger's transparencies and shipped them all off to New York. I think they used three of Feininger's photographs. I never asked him whether he thought the trip was worth the effort. For me, it was an experience I'd never forget.

By a wonderful irony, later in the year, a number of elk hunters were trapped by a sudden blizzard in the forest a few yards north of the Mogollon Rim Road and the photographer Carl Iwasaki and I were assigned to go down and cover the rescue effort. By now, it was bitter cold, near zero at night, and the Rim Road was deep with snow. We got there just before dark and spent the night numb with cold in one of the sheriff's cars. In the morning, the tracked snow vehicles broke a trail deep into the woods. The hunters were sitting comfortably around a fire. They'd run low on some supplies and had stamped out a message in the snow. Wanting to conserve their energy, they'd stamped out "MJB" instead of "coffee." As the sheriff reached the hunters, one of them said, "If you guys will just break the trail a few hundred yards further up the ridge, we know there's elk back in there." To which the sheriff replied, "Haul your butts out of here while you can." It wasn't quite a nonstory; as I recall, we ran a picture Carl took of the "MJB" in the snow. But, against all odds, I'd gotten to see the Mogollon Rim again.

As *Life* bureaus go (or went), Denver was not ideal. There were stories to be found, but the editors of both *Time* and *Life* in New York had what you might call a "coastal perspective" and it was very hard to interest them in the doings of the Rocky Mountain Empire. As Ed Ogle once remarked, the Cheyenne Roundup—a major rodeo— seemed to come along faster every year.

And yet I found stories that were a pleasure to do. A young string quartet just out of Julliard was vacationing one summer in the mountains and giving what proved to be enchanting lecture concerts to children. They named themselves the LaSalle String Quartet after the street Julliard was on in Manhattan. The LaSalle was my introduction to the sometimes austere joys of chamber music. They became the quartet in residence at the Cincinnati Conservatory and we stayed in touch for years.

I covered a spectacular kayak race down the white water of the Arkansas River at Salida, Colorado. There were, as well, some fascinating personalities in Denver. One was the poet Thomas Hornsby Ferrill, whose host of friends and visitors ranged from Carl Sandburg to Thomas Wolfe, and whose wife, Helen, and daughter, Anne Folsom, had written an amusing book entitled *The Indoor Bird Watcher's Manual.* And, among others, there was the amateur naturalist Walker van Riper, who rigged an ingenious setup for photographing rattlesnakes just as they struck at his camera lens.

But all interesting things come to an end. After two years, Irene called again and said, that was it—I was to please come back to New York and write.

New York Again

So, on a frosty fall day in 1954, I was heading back to the office where I'd begun, but now as a writer. I'd be doing those captions and text blocks that Carvell Collins at Harvard had mentioned with so much amusement when he told me about the possible job at *Life.*

I was now a commuter. Peg and I had found a lovely house on a shady suburban street in White Plains in Westchester County and there our second daughter, Judi, was born. I did my commuting on the New York Central. One of my fellow commuters was Bosley Crowther, the fine film critic of the *New York Times.* Several years later when I was reviewing for the *Los Angeles Times,* we had lunch to compare notes on the stresses and triumphs of the conspicuous roles we played.

As I was shortly to discover, being a writer at *Life* meant being part writer, part mathematician, part literary carpenter. The central frustration of writing for the magazine was that the designers ruled that all paragraphs and captions had to square; that is, there could be no widows or partial lines. In those precomputer days the rules led to a whole process of making things fit squarely. It could be hell on a Saturday night, as the magazine was going to press, when you were told that a caption, already mercilessly squeezed, needed five more characters removed—and there was no way you could see to do it.

My first writing assignment was simple. A "fast color page," which took only a week longer than the black-and-white pages to be engraved, had been laid out. The picture was of a mountain rescue, which needed just a few lines of explanatory text. But I crumpled up some twenty sheets of copy paper before I achieved what I thought was a proper blend of accuracy and drama.

About the time *Life* started in 1936, founder Henry Luce sent a brief message to his writers: "Never underestimate the reader's intelligence and never overestimate his information." That was one of the stars I sailed by.

In my trainee days, I'd stood many times in the office of Managing Editor Ed Thompson sound-tracking the story he was looking at. Now I watched the procedure as a writer. After Ed had decided on a layout, I'd go back to my desk to read the newspaper clippings and research the correspondent had put together as background for the text I was going to write.

In no time at all, I'd receive a large photocopy of the layout with dummy type in place and indications of how long everything should be. Text blocks were often 69 characters wide and the captions more often than not were two lines of 47 characters. Those and many other sizes are embedded so deeply in my memory that I'll never be able to forget them.

The progress of the story led me to another of those extraordinary men who were to have a tremendous impact on my work as a writer. Joseph Kastner was *Life*'s copy editor, a burly man with pale red hair who'd begun his Time, Inc., career as a writer at *Fortune*. Above all, Joe knew his own mind in all things. He was the first on the magazine's staff to own one of the new Volkswagen Bugs and was chided for acquiring such a bizarre vehicle. But he was soon acknowledged as a prophet.

Joe had a small office next door to the managing editor's. There, armed with a large jar of freshly sharpened No. 2 pencils, he read every piece of copy that appeared in the magazine. When your story had been typed in the copy room and distributed Joe would call you into his office and invariably you arrived with your stomach knotted. Often, in the beginning, he would discuss where you went wrong and send you back to your office to try again. On your next visit you could watch him pencil-edit the new version on a sheet of flimsy yellow paper. When he scrawled his "J. K." on the sheet, you'd passed the first hurdle.

Now the freshly typed and edited copy came back to you with arcane markings in the margins. These were your clues to keeping the copy square. The copyreaders might say "Green 3 lines" if your story was overlong, or "Green 10–15, some small" if the caption might require adjustment. To give the typesetters some flexibility, you were to mark in brackets which characters could be left in, added to, or removed without changing the sense of the copy. The computer would make all this unnecessary but, alas, that would be after my time.

One frustrating, treasonable night, a fellow writer carefully typed out the Gettysburg Address on a sheet of copy paper, added the marginal marking "green 5 lines," and then marked the copy with brackets indicating how it could be done. The new version began "In 1776," instead of "Fourscore and seven," a great saving. And so it went down to the great conclusion, "People's government won't die." It'd been a long, long night.

There was one last hurdle for our copy to get over. Ed Thompson had to approve the final version and scrawl his "E. K. T." on the copy. It was a particular triumph to get your "E. K. T." on a headline. Headlines had to convey a great deal in a few characters. The most glorious triumph of my whole *Life* writing career involved one 9.5-character headline. It was for a Picture of the Week which an amateur had taken from his boat of another fisherman in the next boat. The fisherman had hooked a big pike and you could see the still-bent pole and the pike in midair. But the pike had somehow spat out the hook and you could see the hook as well. It was an amazing shot, one of the greatest Pictures of the Week. It fell to me to write it and I came up with a headline that read "PIKES PIQUE." The copy desk said, too bad, the headline was a half character too long, or something like that. I was crestfallen. Joe Kastner was crestfallen. Ed Thompson was crestfallen. He commanded the production people to do something magical with the layout so my headline would fit. Never again would I experience quite the same sense of power over a layout.

One night, my colleague Loudon Wainwright was writing a sports story and having a headline problem—the problem being Ed Thompson, who rejected every headline Loudon suggested. Loudon typed a note and pinned it to the cork wall above his typewriter: "How can he be so sure what he wants and not know what it is?"

Kastner reached the office at ten in the morning, as we all did, and was still there late at night, as we all were. One particularly long night, one of my colleagues said, "If you put a hamburger in front of Joe just now, he would edit it." After his retirement, Joe revealed what an excellent writer he was himself. He became an expert on American naturalists and published a book and many articles. What Kastner demonstrated to me week after week, during five years' worth of his patient perusing, was that there was nothing that couldn't be said more simply and more tightly, yet also with something like eloquence and grace.

Often after one of the hectic late closings, some of us would feel too wired up to head home. We needed a drink and a chance to talk a little treason. One night, Michael Arlen, a researcher at the magazine and the son of the author of *The Green Hat*, one of the great best sellers of the 1920s, led a small group of the night's survivors to Place Elegante, an after-hours bar in a grand old brownstone house on East 56th Street. There was a handsome circular staircase greeting you inside the front door and it led to a mezzanine, where an ancient piano player provided background music, ranging from Rodgers and Hart to the fight songs of all the better Ivy League colleges. Time seemed to have stood still at the Elegante. Scott and Zelda were long gone, but it wouldn't have been surprising, especially after a martini or two in the late-night hours, to catch sight of their ghosts coming through the door, or arguing at a table in a dark corner of the mezzanine. I felt like a time traveler carried back to the 1920s, when the Elegante might well have been a fancy speakeasy.

It was on one of those nights that I told myself, "You are where you belong. This should be your world. The writer, having written, has earned that late-hour martini and the company of beautiful and handsome friends."

My office for five years was room 31-11, with a view toward the East River. I shared the office most of the time with a bulky, bald, cigar-smoking master of applied whimsy named David Snell. Like Harry Truman he had no middle name, not even an initial.

Dave had been an editorial cartoonist and reporter on the *World-Telegram* before he was hired by *Life*. He was from Minden, Louisiana, where his father owned a cotton gin. Dave went to LSU and wrestled there, becoming for a time a professional wrestler—the "Masked Villain"—after he graduated. I came to know him as a man who lived under considerable stress, which he revealed inadvertently, but never discussed. Whatever was going on in his mind and soul he concealed with his great physical energy and unique gift for tomfoolery. At one point, he took up sign painting and was very good at it. At other times, he became intensely devoted to ceramics and making jewelry from copper. There were few of us who didn't have a coffee cup adorned with one of his cartoons. His men all looked like close relatives, bald and desperately sad-eyed, with large, down-curling, melancholy lips. One of his cartoons showed an electric cord running from a wall plug to the lights on a Christmas tree, with a spur leading to an electric chair on which sat one of Dave's characteristic men awaiting his fate in melancholy gloom. I was never sure whether Dave's men were conscious caricatures of himself, but they could have been.

Having long ago discovered that "Hotel Plunge" just fit the one-column measure in the tabloid papers, the *Daily Mirror* and the *Daily News,* Dave painted a "Hotel Plunge" sign and taped it over the door to 31-11. Over the years, he clipped every headline he could find that included those two words: "Sailor Dies in Hotel Plunge," "Tourist Dies in Hotel Plunge," and so on. He must have had two dozen of them in various shades of yellowing.

Our furnishings consisted of desks and a large work table, to which I added an amplifier, a turntable, and a number of records; Dave added an oilcloth tablecloth. Because of the late closings, every Saturday night, Time, Inc. supplied a dinner catered by the Louis XIV restaurant in Rockefeller Center. There being no objections, we occasionally had wine and a candle to add to the festivity. Room 31-11 became the place to have dinner on Saturday night, and there are colleagues these fifty-odd years later who speak of dinner at the "Hotel Plunge" as others might remember a meal at 21.

Nonsense was Dave's forte. One day, he discovered a large map of the United States, one of those maps with plastic bumps indicating mountains. It was about to be tossed out as junk. Dave rescued it, printed a legend in a clear stretch of the Pacific saying "Map Showing Location of Colored Pins," filled the map with red- and white-colored pins, and hung it up in our office. When he worked at the *World-Telegram,* he'd done a favor for a man who made rubber stamps and, ever after, the man would make any stamp Dave wanted. One of his favorites was "Whoever did this will report to Miss Agatha Fangquill in Room 210." Whenever an interoffice memo struck Dave as especially fatuous, he'd give it Miss Fangquill's stamp of disapproval and send it on. Miss Fangquill was a true sister to the Snell men, except that she had more hair. Dave had other stamps with long, postcard-filling messages over the signature of Justice of the Peace W. P. Spillage.

He was an eccentric collector. What seemed to be an old-fashioned crank telephone on the wall turned out to be a radio. In a story told by Dick Starnes, Dave's editor at the *World Telegram*, not long after Dave had defected to *Life*, the telephone system at the newspaper was being replaced. One of the lads looked at the great wiry tangles of discarded equipment and cried, "Hey, Dave's back!"

When he received his first writing assignment, Dave hunched into his typewriter, his chin almost touching the keyboard, staring at the paper as if the words would appear as from a secret message. When he was called to the copy editor's office for guidance on a rewrite he would storm back to the office, say nothing to me or anyone else who happened to be there, and hunch over the typewriter again, as if his job at the magazine was in jeopardy. It wasn't. Not only did he quickly become one of the best writers at *Life*, he later became a copy editor, renowned for his gentle touch.

Dave was somewhat improbably assigned to the Paris bureau, improbably because, despite his Louisiana heritage, he had no ear for French. For six weeks before he left, he took a marathon course at Berlitz, returning to the office haggard with the strain. When he finished the course, he told us, "Wait 'til they have a press conference about pencils. I'll be over it like a tent." He had his enormous blue Chrysler convertible, which he called the "May Basket," shipped over to him, and there were legends about his valiant attempts to steer it along the narrow French streets.

When *Life* died, Dave set up shop in Houston as a freelancer, specializing in medical stories. His sense of whimsy lived on in his letters, sometimes recounting the further adventures of Judge Spillage, sometimes arriving in envelopes marked "Bates School of Motel Management." I hadn't seen Dave for years when I got word that he'd fallen ill. I flew down to see him in the hospital. We spent the better part of an afternoon remembering Miss Fangquill and the Hotel Plunge, and then we said good-bye.

In the early days, most of my writing was still unsigned, but I did have two pieces, brief but with a signature at the bottom. One was a piece on the riotous party that marked the closing of the original Toots Shor's restaurant in New York. It was black tie and all of Shor's so-called pals came to do honor to the great man, who passed out and was carted off around two in the morning. It was that kind of a party. I was the only one there I didn't know. It was my first meeting with John Wayne, but it would not be my last, and I always felt a great affection for him.

My other signed piece was on the Spring Hill mine disaster, another of the rare occasions when I abandoned my desk for the outside world.

One afternoon, the wire services reported that several men presumed dead in a mine cave-in in Nova Scotia were in fact still alive. Faint tappings had been heard. Alfred Eisenstaedt and I and two other reporter-photographer teams rushed to the airport, not pausing for toothbrushes. We flew to Boston and boarded a chartered plane for Halifax. When the Halifax airport was shut down because of fog, we flew on to an abandoned Royal Canadian Air Force landing field, where a rental car awaited us. I was elected to drive and we took off on a narrow two-lane macadam road in the rain and fog. I steered by the white line at the edge of the road, swerving as the road curved abruptly. "Go slower, child," Eisie kept saying. "Better we get there late than not at all." We made it just after dawn, and I said I was going over to the hospital where the first survivor was being examined. Eisie said he'd go with me. The man's family was gathered around him in the ward and his granddaughter, not more than three, had been plunked down on his chest. She leaned forward to feel his grizzled beard and I thought, "That's one hell of a picture. Where's

WITH JOHN WAYNE: *The Duke and I chatting at a party at the closing of the old Toots Shor's restaurant in New York, in 1959. Photo by Bill Ray,* Life *magazine.*

Eisie?" At that moment, I heard a faint click behind me. Eisie had the picture. It dominated the story *Life* ran.

Eisenstaedt was the nearest to an authentic instinctive genius of any of the photographers I knew and worked with. He didn't waste a frame. When he saw a picture in his viewfinder, he took it. The legend was that he did his first three stories for *Life* on one roll of 35 mm film. He and his camera had an almost organic relationship. A camera was always around his neck; as he moved from one condition of light to the next, his fingers almost automatically adjusted his lens aperture or shutter speed so that he was forever ready to shoot. He'd been a button salesman in Germany in the early 1920s when he bought his first Leica and discovered his true calling. He was short, balding, and gnomish. He knew how good he was and expected first-cabin treatment.

One year, he was assigned to do a color essay on the Everglades. Leaving New York, he was furious because no staff person was going with him and no correspondent was going to meet him. He wasn't even going to be helped by a stringer, but by a stringer's wife. As it turned out, the wife was a stunningly pretty blonde and Eisie always enjoyed pretty women. She was also marvelously efficient. If Eisie said he wished there were a snake behind a lily pad, quite by chance, there'd be a snake there, which increased Eisie's admiration of the lady.

Back in New York, he sang her praises; standing in the news bureau he said, "I think I will send her some chocolates." Everyone was amazed that he was going to do something by himself, but, after a pause, he looked around and asked, "Who's in charge of sending out chocolates?"

Eisie was a superb portraitist, who shot dozens of covers for *Life*. Sophia Loren liked the way Eisie made her look and she never wanted to be photographed by anyone else. When I did an interview with her years later, she talked about Eisie as you might an adored sweetheart. He shot his portraits with a relatively long lens so that he crouched well across the room from his subject and was not, to borrow a phrase, in their faces.

Working at Time, Inc., never stopped being a rich learning experience. In New York, as in Chicago or Denver, there was a rewarding opportunity to read what all of the correspondents were doing. In the bureaus, we saw carbon copies of everything that went back to New York; in New York itself, the information was even more voluminous. Several times a day, a copy messenger stopped by my desk and dropped off a stack of multicolored paper. (I never quite figured out how the color-coding worked.) The papers were copies of everything that came in to New York from the domestic bureaus and occasionally from the foreign bureaus as well. There were one-paragraph traffic messages reporting that shipments of raw film were on their way, but there were also thick stapled "takes" or chapters of a cover story, which made for some wonderful reading. Coles Phinizy, then a deskman in the news system, said jokingly that he lived so far out on Long Island he even had time to get through the takes from the Canadian stringers. The dispatches from Moose Jaw and Yellowknife may not have been compelling reading, but they sometimes stirred up a powerful urge to travel.

From those stacks of papers, I could get a sense of history in the making in Washington, D.C., or a revealing glimpse of Bogart at home in Los Angeles. I still remember the cover story research by Ben Williamson, then the Chicago bureau chief, on the great ballplayer Ted Williams. An image stays in mind from Ben's word portrait of Williams at spring training in Florida—sitting in the dugout reading the *Wall Street Journal.* I encountered a wide range of the American experience: strikes and the reverberations of distant wars, tycoons and the unemployed, parties and customs, crooks and saints, politics and local color. I was reading the work of some of the brightest talents in journalism and, the more I read, the more I learned about what was possible at the height of expository journalism. Amid the anonymity of group journalism, I was proud to realize that some of my own reporting from the bureaus had found its way into those great stacks of colored paper.

There were plenty of stories for me to write at *Life*. The battle for civil rights was raging all through the South and some courageous photographers and reporters were facing the attack dogs, the baton-waving cops, the firehoses: the angry segregationists trying to hold back history. I wrote most of those stories sitting safely in New York, but hoping to convey the strong feelings I had as I read the coverage. Although I'd come back to New York too late to write stories on the first presidential race between Adlai Stevenson and Dwight Eisenhower in 1952, I did quite a number of the magazine's stories about their rematch in 1956. It seemed ironic at the time, and certainly now in retrospect, that one of the most admirable candidates to come along in either party for a long time never really had a chance against the popular general. I first became aware of Stevenson from a small item in *Harpers* magazine. He was then governor of Illinois and the state legislature had passed a bill requiring that cats be kept on leashes. "It is in the nature of cats," he'd pointed out in his veto message, "to do a certain amount of unescorted roaming." When Stevenson appeared on the floor at the Democratic Convention in Los Angeles in 1960, I was part of the Time-Life team covering the excitement. Eleanor Roosevelt introduced him and he received a thunderous ovation. Although Stevenson's name was put in nomination, it was obvious this was his last hurrah. It was a melancholy moment.

After five years in New York, I'd become the senior writer in domestic news, which meant that I wrote most of the big stories. I'd also begun to branch out. I was writing picture essays and I did much of the copy for *Life*'s multipart series "How the West Was Won." Almost every Saturday, I would work late into the night. I was seeing too little of my family and the pressure was getting to me. Finally I went to the new managing editor, a tall, handsome ex-marine named George Hunt and said I'd like to go back to a bureau, any bureau where I could be used, but that, given my druthers, my preference was Los Angeles. I'd always been fond of the movies, and while television was stealing away moviegoers by the millions, it seemed that movies still had a tremendous influence on society everywhere. Somewhat reluctantly, George said he'd arrange for me to work in the Los Angeles bureau—and so began an important part of my writing life.

Welcome to L.A.

I flew into Los Angeles on a fiercely hot, dry, gritty, and smoggy day in August 1959. From the descending plane, the city seemed to be covered by a transparent brown blanket.

A close friend and fellow commuter in New York days, Art Seidenbaum, was now in the L.A. office (which was more precisely in Beverly Hills). Art and John Jenkisson, the *Life* bureau chief, came down to the airport to pick me up.

Working at the magazine was in a sense like joining a club whose members came together for a time and parted and then met again in some other corner of the country or the world. I had the feeling that it was like being a minor consul for the State Department. Seidenbaum and I had commuted from Westchester to Manhattan and now we would commute to Beverly Hills.

Art and John deposited me at the Cavalier Motel, where *Time* and *Life* stashed their visitors and other new hands. The Cavalier is long gone and the site now holds one of the high-rising and high-priced condominium towers that make that stretch of Wilshire Boulevard a dark canyon much of the time.

I'd never been in Los Angeles and yet the city seemed familiar. I'd come to know its streets, bright or menacing, from the work of detective writers, especially Raymond Chandler. Ah, yes, La Cienega, Wilshire, Santa Monica Boulevard. As Art drove us north on Sepulveda—another of those familiar names—I glimpsed the water tower with the large letters "MGM" on it. Whatever else was true, I knew I'd come to the right place.

I realized that Los Angeles had been one large movie set almost from the moment the cameras started rolling, hand-cranked, at the turn of the century. Millions of us had been lured west by the images of the Keystone Kops cavorting on the beaches or Buster Keaton driving a horse and precariously loaded wagon along one of the boulevards. Perhaps even more attractive, and envied and copied across the country, were the sunlit bungalows that stretched out invitingly from the ocean to the mountains.

The city was partly an oasis of glamour, but it was also a place of hope for all those who'd been displaced and driven west by the Dust Bowl of the 1930s. The movies had given us that, too, in that classic drama of social realism *The Grapes of Wrath*.

At the Cavalier, that very first afternoon, I unpacked my Olivetti portable. One of my ambitions had been to begin a novel immediately and I may have been so brazen as to type "Chapter One" on a piece of yellow paper. I'd been given a ground-floor room near the swimming pool. As I sat at the open window, two men walked by outside. I suspected they were visitors as well, and probably movie marketing executives. One of them said, "Eddie got me a date for the night with that really sexy usherette." "Wow," the other man said, as he moved out of earshot. That dates my story; usherettes are an extinct species.

Not for the last time, I said to myself, "Welcome to Hollywood."

That night John Jenkisson gave me a welcoming party at his home on a cul-de-sac off Benedict Canyon. I'd rented a car and somehow found my way. John introduced me to something he called the "Swiss Itch," which consisted of some salt from the back of your hand followed by a shot of tequila and a suck of lime. (As I'd later learn, that was the way most everyone drank straight tequila.)

The next day was Sunday and after a restorative sleep I began my exploration of the city, concluding at dusk up on Mulholland Drive, which snakes along the crest of the Santa Monica Mountains. To the north, the lights of the San Fernando Valley stretched all the way to the next mountains. In the other direction, the lights of the Los Angeles basin ran south as far as I could see. The vision in both directions was of a golden carpet of incandescence, a romantic phrase that occurred to me as I drove slowly along. The lights concealed the miles of the mean streets Raymond Chandler wrote about and the countless shopping centers. It was only after I'd been in town for a while that I came to see that, in its lateral sprawl, Los Angeles offered more decent living space to more people over a wider range of income than any city I knew.

On Monday morning, I checked into the bureau, which was a floor in a small office building on Little Santa Monica Boulevard in the heart of Beverly Hills. Jim Murray, who became the best-loved sports writer in the country, was on the *Time* side. He contributed to the dummy issues of a magazine called "MNORX," which spaced out like *SPORT*, a title Time, Inc., was trying to acquire but never did. So the magazine became *Sports Illustrated*. In the meantime, Jim went off to the *Los Angeles Times*.

Shana Alexander was one of the *Life* correspondents, on her way to become a major columnist and one of the anchors on *60 Minutes*. The *Time* bureau chief was Frank McCullough, a veteran newsman and an aggressive, insightful reporter. Dave Zeitlin was *Life*'s Hollywood correspondent and Bob Jennings, a soft-voiced Southerner, covered showbiz for *Time*. Although my goal was to write about the movies myself, at the moment, I was a general assignment correspondent, glad to be in Los Angeles in any role.

At first I house-sat for Ralph Crane, one of the *Life* photographers who was on a month's vacation. By the time Ralph reclaimed his house, I'd found a permanent home for us on a hill in Pacific Palisades with a view of the Pacific. Our neighbors included Joseph Cotten and his wife, Patricia Medina, who had a large manor at the bottom of our street, and the old silent idol, Francis X. Bushman, whom we often saw out for a walk looking the picture of stately dignity. The house was on a cul-de-sac named Giardino Way, about ten miles from Beverly Hills and I acquired a faithful VW Bug for the commute. While there, our fifth child arrived, a splendid daughter named Susan. (In the end, our six children would be born in four states and two countries.)

Once I'd settled into the bureau, I could in a sense look around at the country and the world as well as Southern California. It was, as became dramatically clear in the passing months, a turning point for the country. Eisenhower was completing his second and final term as president; 1959 had already been a year of much presidential political activity. In the new year, the Republicans nominated Richard Nixon. On the Democratic side, there was fierce rivalry between Lyndon Johnson and John Fitzgerald Kennedy. One night photographer John Bryson and I drove out to Orange County where Senator Kennedy had flown in from Washington for a whistle-stop visit. We took pictures of him kissing a baby or two in the great tradition of candidates for office. Kennedy had left Washington at three in the morning Los Angeles time and had spent an exhausting day invading what was thought to be heavily Republican Orange County. Late that night, Joe Serrell, a Democratic worker, told me that he'd just said good night to the candidate in his suite at the Disneyland Hotel. Kennedy's ailing back was killing him. Sitting in a rocking chair, which occasionally gave him relief, he'd shut his eyes and said, "Joe, tell me this is all worth it."

I did a great deal of political reporting, following the various state delegations for clues as to whether they would go for Johnson or for Kennedy when the balloting began on the Convention floor. When Kennedy emerged as the presidential nominee we all felt a surge of excitement. The campaign was a high hurdle for the first Catholic nominee since Al Smith. When he won in November, there seemed no doubt a new era had begun for the country, what we came to think of as the Camelot years.

Ralph Crane had taken a beautiful, symbolic picture summing up the Hollywood of that moment. It was of a jackrabbit staring insolently at the camera on the back lot of Twentieth Century Fox, which the rabbit seemed to have all to itself. The studio, like the industry, was suffering, but Fox more than most. Television was stealing Hollywood's audiences at a fast clip. Fox's notorious production of *Cleopatra* with Elizabeth Taylor and Richard Burton, whose blazing new romance made headlines almost hourly, was draining the studio's fiscal resources, so that bankruptcy was a real possibility. Fox was also shooting *Can-Can*, an expensive musical shortly to be inspected by Nikita Khrushchev, the Soviet premier on his historic visit to the United States. I watched him visibly enjoying the dancing girls, but when he got back to Russia, he denounced the film as another example of "Western decadence."

The day after *Can-Can*, Khrushchev boarded a special train for San Francisco along with several hundred journalists, of whom I was one. The train was to leave at nine in the morning. I realized almost too late that I'd never driven from Santa Monica to Union Station downtown and had only the vaguest idea where it was. There was then no Santa Monica Freeway, so I was making the best time I could on the surface streets. But I managed to find a parking place at the station and got aboard the train almost as it started to move. The ride suggested a sequence from a Jacques Tati movie. At every stop, Khrushchev got off the train to shake a few hands in the crowd pressed against the fences at the station. And when he got off, of course, all the reporters piled off, too. When he reboarded the train, there was a mad dash by the thundering reporters to get back on the train before it started moving. Khrushchev made his way through all the cars shaking hands with the press. One of the reporters, who'd served in Russia for the *New York Times,* I believe, had his son with him. Reminding Khrushchev he'd been in Moscow as one of those hated Western journalists, he put an arm around his son and said he hoped the sins of the father would not be visited on the son. Khrushchev smiled but said neither should the sins be forgotten. It was a curious little playlet, with as many undertones as you cared to hear.

Khrushchev, whom his translator referred to as "The Chairman," presumably did not see the jackrabbit inhabiting the Fox back lot, and I'm not sure he learned much about Hollywood. But the whole life of Hollywood can be seen as a kind of prolonged game of Russian Roulette, except that the revolver's chamber is always empty. Its financial ups and downs are never predictable but, in the end, are never fatal either. Fox had been having more than its share of troubles, but the slyest fox of all, Darrell F. Zanuck, rode to the rescue. He personally produced the all-star, black-and-white movie *The Longest Day,* based on the book of the same title by Cornelius Ryan about D-Day. The movie was a huge success and kept Fox afloat. As a nice irony, *Cleopatra* wound up in the black, too. Still, when Fox sold off the back lot, jackrabbit and all, to Alcoa, it betokened a changing day in Hollywood. Alcoa then built Century City, whose shiny buildings have become the legal and financial center of Los Angeles. At about the same time, MGM sold off its own legendary back lot for a housing development whose subdivisions had names like "Raintree County."

I'd missed much of Hollywood's golden age, but luckily I was there in time to view the last days of the back lots. They were deserted and it was eerie in the late hours of an afternoon to walk alone through what seemed like a geographic phantasmagoria, in which the façade of one or two brownstone houses out of turn-of-the-century New York stood almost cheek by jowl with the façade of the waterfront saloon of a French fishing village. There were even traces of the jungle where Tarzan yelled his famous yell and I spotted the clapboard home where dwelt Judge Hardy and his son Andy.

I did a magazine piece about the back lots and the melancholy sense of their past and my own. I even wrote about an idea I had for a thriller involving some murders on a back lot which turned out to be the work of a former small-time actor who'd gone bonkers for lack of work and was now living as a hermit among the niches and shadows of the partial buildings. I think it's just as well for literature that I never got around to writing it.

In the next several months, I covered a strike by film writers, concentrating on the desperate rush to finish some films before the strike began. One of them was *Dark at the Top of the Stairs,* starring Dorothy McGuire. I covered a rescue on Mount McKinley and the first-ever taking of the census on Hawaii as a state. We visited all of the major islands except the privately owned island of Niihau. We had hoped to reach it by the regular supply boat, but we were stopped at the dock at dawn by guards with rifles. Back in California, a photographer and I rented a light plane to photograph that summer's raging forest fires. I kept nudging him and saying, "Look down there!" But he was so engrossed in the new James Bond book that he put it down only with the greatest reluctance.

I inherited what sounded like an exciting story. Some trials for hydroplane racers (those wide, flat, high-powered boats that look like oversized flounders) were going to be held for the first time on Lake Mead in Arizona. Ralph Crane and I reconnoitered the lake in a launch. He decided that the ideal place from which to shoot was a small undeveloped outcrop of lava rock well out from the shore. On the first day, I lugged what seemed like several hundred pounds of photographic equipment, splashing through the water from the launch to the rock, there being no dock. Hydroplanes are quite susceptible to flipping over backward if there is much more than a ripple on the surface of the water. There were small waves that first day, so the trials were cancelled and I lugged all that equipment back through the water to the launch. The next day the same thing happened—lug, set up, wait, cancellation. By now, I was having trouble standing erect. My back was in full protest. The third day was a repetition of the first two, except by now the officials decided that Lake Mead wasn't going to work, so the trials were cancelled altogether. I managed to load the gear one more time, unload it ashore, and then retired to my motel to chew aspirin and try to sleep.

The lesson of this saga was that I was not in shape to be a Sherpa bearer and probably too old to be a reporter in the field. I decided I wanted to switch to the *Time* side of the bureau. This required some delicacy. *Life* was quite possessive about its people and looked unkindly on people switching over to *Time*. I took the problem to the adroit chief of all Time-Life correspondents, Dick Clurman. He went to the managing editor of *Life*, George Hunt. "Chuck doesn't want to leave *Life*," Clurman told George, his fingers crossed, "but *Time* needs him badly," his fingers still crossed. Hunt agreed that *Time* could have me. I didn't even have to change my desk. I simply started dealing first, last, and always with my preferred medium, words.

It follows that anyone with a passionate love of words and writing would have a special fascination about talking with writers. So it was that three of my most enjoyable assignments at *Time* in Los Angeles involved writers.

I knew that Will and Ariel Durant lived in Los Angeles, but they seemed as remote from everyday Los Angeles life as fishermen on an island off Scotland. So far as I knew, they didn't do book signings, and they didn't appear on radio shows or television. They just researched and wrote. Their scholarly dedication to the project that had consumed them for more than thirty years—their unprecedented multivolume study of people and ideas, *The Story of Civiliza-*

tion—had always seemed to me to represent the ultimate ideal of a writing career. Then, in 1961, the magazine asked me to seek out an interview with the Durants, who'd just published the seventh volume, *The Age of Reason Begins*. In it, Will Durant wrote, "Barring some lethal surprise to the authors or to civilization," there would be two more volumes, *The Age of Louis XIV*, in 1963, and *The Age of Voltaire*, in 1965. As it happened, there were three additional volumes before Will Durant's death. Commencing with *The Age of Reason Begins*, Will insisted that Ariel share the authorship credit with him.

I found that the Durants lived in an imposing two-story house with a Cadillac in the garage, high in the Hollywood Hills. Durant was small, quiet, and the very model of a scholar. His wife, Ariel, was petite and as outspoken as her husband was not. He had met and married her when she was fifteen and one of his students at a progressive school back East. They worked in an upstairs study, Will seated in a rocking chair with a wide board that fitted across the arms of the chair and on which, secured by rubber bands, were two sets of notes on colored paper. Here, in patient longhand (barely legible, Ariel said), he composed the tens of thousands of words of *The Story*. They began work on the earlier volumes only after more than a year's research, the later volumes taking about three years each to complete. Durant estimated that their outline for any one volume would probably run to 600 print pages.

They'd begun their monumental work in 1929 and it quickly became one of the all-time nonfiction publishing successes. The Book-of-the-Month Club had distributed, as we spoke, more than 120,000 sets of *The Story of Civilization* as a book dividend or an inducement to join the Club. Those were in addition to some 60,000 copies of each volume sold in the United States alone.

Ariel sat on a couch opposite Will and their process of composition seemed a sort of wonderfully enriched conversation. She was obviously a writer's dream of a zealous researcher, supplementing Will's vision of the past with a flood of dates, brief biographies, and a profusion of facts. Although they'd already been amply rewarded, they continued to work with total dedication: beginning at eight in the morning, breaking at noon for lunch and a short nap for Will, resuming later in the afternoon, breaking again for dinner, and going back to work in the evening. Ariel was deep into Gibbon's *Decline and Fall of the Roman Empire* for the next volume. Gibbon, she noted, had longed to have a few years after completing his great work simply to enjoy it. "We know just how he felt," she said. Fortunately, they did have time to enjoy their achievement before Will died in 1981.

Durant was often identified as a popularizer of intellectual history, but, in fact, he was a deeply serious scholar with a remarkable gift for synthesizing a wealth of research material into a readable story. What remains vividly in my memory is the image of this soft-voiced man and his adoring wife who made the past live because it lived for them in all its triumphs, cruelties, discoveries, and persisting hopes.

It seemed to me then, as it does in memory, that the Durants were diminutive people who wrote like giants and who created a work of genius that will live beyond them for many, many years.

In the spring of 1961, *Time* assigned me to interview the expatriate English novelist Aldous Huxley. This was another expedition to my own past as a reader, an Anglophile, and a literary hero-worshiper about to meet his idol. I'd been reading Huxley's novels since I was in high school. (They were not in the curriculum of course.) I'd read *Eyeless in Gaza, After Many a Summer Dies the Swan,* and *Brave New World,* and some of his short stories, most memorably, "The Giaconda Smile." Huxley had been living in the Hollywood Hills with his vivacious red-haired wife, Laura, when their house had burned to the ground in the brush fires that had swept through.

I tracked him down to a Hollywood hotel, where they were living temporarily.

He'd managed to save two suits and the uncompleted manuscript of his new novel, *Island,* about a utopian community, which represented several years' work. The treasures he'd lost included the original manuscripts of all his books, except for *Brave New World,* which was in the University of Texas archives. "It's terribly frustrating," Huxley said, "to find yourself with no shirts, no undershirts, no socks, no toothbrush, all the things one takes for granted."

What was most dismaying to Huxley was that he'd lost all his books, his correspondence, including all his letters from his first wife, and his address books. "The whole record of my past is gone. I've forgotten everyone's address and I fear it will take me a long time to reconstruct them. One doesn't know where to begin."

As I always remember the Durants sitting in their den in their extraordinary collaboration, I continue to remember Huxley as he stood talking to me with a look of haunted bereavement, thinking about all the people he'd known over a long life. His friends, men and women alike, were a rich sampling of the world's thinkers and doers.

Huxley died in 1963. He was an idol I'd met in the nick of time. I was able to thank the man who wrote all those insightful novels I'd started reading in my late adolescence, particularly *Chrome Yellow* and *Antic Hay.*

Another distinguished expatriate writer in our midst in Los Angeles was Christopher Isherwood. *Time* assigned me to interview him about his new novel, *Down There on a Visit.* Isherwood lived deep in Santa Monica Canyon, just above the ocean, with his companion, the artist Don Bacardy. A long, steep flight of concrete steps led down from Adelaide Drive to Isherwood's house. Unfortunately, I'd broken my leg a few weeks earlier playing touch football, a highly patriotic activity in the Kennedy years, with a group of us from the Time-Life office and my right leg was in a long cast. When I got to the top of the steps, it began to pour, always rare in Los Angeles. I realized there was no way I could descend the steps on my crutches, so I sat on the first step and bumped my way down, step by step, to the front door.

Isherwood, an enormously kind man, was appalled at the sight of me, drenched as I was, but I sat on some newspapers to spare his furniture and we had what turned out to be a charming conversation. When he arrived from England with the poet W. H. Auden in 1939, Isherwood joined a small group of Britons in exile, most of them living in the Santa Monica Canyon, including the novelist Gerald Heard. Isherwood had a brief and predictably frustrating encounter with Hollywood. Writing for the movies proved not to be his métier. After some volunteer work during the war, he became a teacher of literature and writing on various campuses in Southern California, principally at Cal State, Los Angeles.

He'd brought a distinguished literary reputation with him, especially for his Berlin stories, which became the play *I Am a Camera*. Whatever else he was doing, he wrote constantly, converting his life into thinly disguised fiction.

As I sat drying off in his living room, he showed me a bulky volume of handwritten pages, the journal he'd kept most of his adult life. His novels going back to the Berlin years were hewn from the pages of the journal. That is particularly true of *Down There on a Visit*, in which Isherwood revisits various episodes in his life, from Berlin forward. Simply stated, the book investigates the paradox that, though we are always changing, we are always the same living being. As Isherwood says in the novel, "Who am I but a daily succession of statements to a mirror that I am I?"

Some of my most satisfying writing has been drawn from my own life, as in my memoir, *Back There Where the Past Was*. Isherwood's special appeal to me was that he wrote such moving and insightful fiction from the nonfiction of his life. I've almost never written fiction, but I've found particular satisfaction in trying to put my own life in perspective as Christopher Isherwood did.

On the basis of the files I sent to New York on Huxley and Isherwood, someone in the News Bureau concluded that I got on well with English people, or words to that effect. For that reason or any other, I was told late in 1961 that, if I wanted to, I could go work in the London bureau of *Time* in mid-1962. If I wanted to! I could think of no more exciting and challenging assignment.

Home to England

The England to which I came in the summer of 1962 was no longer the capital of an empire on which the sun never set. There was no longer an empire. England had freed the last of its great colonies, India, in 1947. Now Great Britain was at the head of a commonwealth of independent countries, joined to the mother country by ancient ties of tradition, trade, and a common language. But if it was an England newly defined, it was a strong and imposing voice among the nations of the world, one that still spoke with a moral authority far beyond its earthly powers.

My expectation when I set off for England was that my return would be a homecoming. I'd only been in England twice. The first time, I'd arrived in Liverpool at night by ship from Boston and glimpsed Southampton the next day before boarding an LST for the Channel crossing to Le Havre. The second time I was flown as a wounded private from Aachen, Germany, to Cheltenham and the 128th General Hospital. But my attachment to England was long and deep.

I'd been an Anglophile before I was old enough to know what the word meant. Sherlock Holmes was my first detective hero; from him, or from Conan Doyle, forward, I was drawn to English literature like an iron filing to a magnet. The Dickens and the Sir Walter Scott we read in school may have been a burdensome bother to my classmates, but not to me. I loved every colorfully romantic word.

Well before I graduated from high school, I'd consumed whole chunks of Graham Greene's "Entertainments," like *This Gun for Hire.* Great Aunt Caroline, who'd died years before I was born, had bought a complete Dickens in thirty-six volumes. The pages in many of the volumes were still uncut when I set about reading most of the better-known novels, including *The Pickwick Papers.* Empire or no empire, I felt that I'd truly come home to England. I don't know how I could have been more steeped in the idea of life in England without actually bathing in tea.

I did not expect to live in the England of Charles Dickens, but I did expect the England of Graham Greene, and that's what I found: a world that could be both elegantly classy and working-class comfortable.

We sailed to England on the last great American ocean liner, the SS *United States.* I was the only one of my family who escaped sea-sickness during the rough early going. Then the seas calmed and our children enjoyed the run of the ship. Each day, the ship distributed a one-sheet news update. The bulletin on August 23rd, that Marilyn Monroe had died unexpectedly in Hollywood, took the bloom off the rest of the cruise for me. I'd never met her and yet she had that peculiar fascination for many of us men, who thought of her not just as a sex symbol but as a vulnerable woman whom we had wanted to protect and know better.

We stopped first at Le Havre, where the British immigration offi-cials came aboard. They were questioning, very politely, whether I could enter the United Kingdom as a working journalist. Even as they checked their thick book of regulations, the radio operator came in with a teletype from the London bureau saying cryptically, "Enter as tourists." For a brief moment, I felt like a wartime displaced per-son whose papers were not in order. The office later explained that it had forgotten to register me at the Home Office.

We docked in Southampton, fittingly for a wet country, in the pouring rain. Smelling of wet wool, the seven of us crammed into a

Rover sedan driven by the office's chauffeur, Joe Patterson, and made our slow way to London through the continuing downpour.

The actual England of 1962 did not entirely conform to the England of my fantasies. There were still remnants of the war and the bombings to be seen, vacant lots with foundations still visible, excavations piled high with rubble. Rationing was still a fresh memory. In the early postwar days, Time, Inc. had contributed to the rebuilding of badly bombed London by erecting its own building on New Bond Street, across from the Westbury Hotel, where I would spend many a pleasing cocktail hour.

The office had leased a furnished flat for us in Kenilworth Court, a red-brick Edwardian block of flats at Putney Bridge. The children were fascinated by the swans, said to be owned by the queen, which swam by in the Thames and waddled up the bank to cadge food. The next morning, I took the Underground to the office for the first time. The Time-Life building was four stories high and we were on the third floor, the ad people on the second. The main floor was leased to Justerini and Brooks, the wine merchant, and to an airline, Varig, as I remember.

The bureau chief was Robert Elson, a tall and imposing figure whom I'd first known when he was an assistant managing editor of *Life*. Bob had aspired to be the editor, but when he saw that it was not to be, the London assignment was a splendid consolation. He'd been city editor of a Vancouver newspaper when he was not yet twenty. An even-handed bureau chief and brilliant correspondent, he quickly developed trusted sources from the prime minister on down.

The doyenne of the correspondents was Honor Balfour, who, in her younger years, had stood unsuccessfully for Parliament as a Liberal candidate at a time when not many Liberals were being elected. She was, without question, the best-informed parliamentary correspondent of them all. Bob Ball covered business for *Time* and *Fortune*. Monica Dehn Wilson was a hearty and beautiful Englishwoman who worked on a variety of stories for *Time*. John Lovesey, who'd come to the bureau as a "school-leaver apprentice," had worked his way up to being the *Sports Illustrated* correspondent. He would later be the sports editor of the *Sunday Times*. Larry Still, another school-leaver apprentice, had a special flair for crimes and trials and would later be a feature writer in those areas for the Vancouver *Sun*. Don Connery, an American like me, was a general assignment correspondent on the *Life* side.

In the large bureaus, there was traditionally something called the "back of the book" correspondent who was responsible for covering all the arts plus a little religion and education, these last to assure that the correspondent's feet stayed on the ground at least some of the time. It was part of my great good fortune that I inherited the "back of the book" beat. The other correspondents were stuck with politics and other disasters, however worthy of attention these might be.

While I was learning my beat and renewing the bureau's contacts with leaders in the arts, Peggy was busy arranging schooling for our four older children. We placed the boys, Chuck and John, in the tough, prestigious Benedict Abbey School in Ealing. It was a long commute involving both the Underground and buses, but the boys found it a daily adventure. *Time* generously paid the school bills. Katy and Judy were enrolled in schools on George Road just off Kingston Hill on the border of Surrey in southwest London, Katy in Marymount International School and Judy in a nearby convent school.

We managed to find a house for sale on George Road just west of the girls' schools—a large Edwardian mansion named Hertcombe that had been divided into two homes. Along with the familiar abbreviation "5 BR," the ad included one I'd never run across before:

"PCH." As we quickly learned, this stood for "part central heating" and meant that part of the house was even colder than the rest. It proved to be one of the coldest winters of the century.

The moving van delivered our furniture on December 7, 1962, a date that will live in our memories, if not in infamy. The movers left about three o'clock, saying they needed to get on the road before the fog rolled in. We had to get back to Kenilworth Court, not least because we had left baby Susan with a sitter whose time was limited. But, by the time we got into the car, the fog was already so thick we couldn't see past the hood. So we set out on foot to grope our way homeward. By now it was dark, too. We walked until we came upon a double-decker bus, virtually the only moving vehicle we'd seen, and hailed it. The driver very nicely showed us the way to go from where we got off at Putney Heath. Whenever one of the children would fall behind in the fog, we'd stop and talk the stray back to us.

Once settled into Hertcombe, I lived the life of a dilettante. My timing was perfect. Postwar Britain was bursting with vitality and optimism. There was a new set of creators who didn't so much cut across class lines as ignore them altogether.

Movies had long been an honored British export. Now they were enjoying a creative rebirth, thanks to the tax subsidies that encouraged film production in Britain. At the same time, there was suddenly such an influx of American filmmakers that my friend Alexander Walker, film critic at the *Daily Standard,* wrote a book about it, *Hollywood, UK.* Some of the younger American movie people started a weekly Sunday morning softball game in Kensington Park. Most nights, restaurants like the White Elephant had more American than British patrons.

A new generation of actors and actresses, including Michael Caine, Peter O'Toole, Tom Courtenay, Sean Connery, and Julie Christie came to prominence. Caine enjoyed a smashing success in *Alfie,* and a bit later in *The Ipcress File.* O'Toole achieved instant star status with his heroic performance in David Lean's *Lawrence of Arabia*. Sean Connery, a Scot who once polished coffins in Glasgow, and who'd gotten his start in show business in the chorus of *South Pacific*, was completing his second James Bond movie, *From Russia with Love*, and the series would make him a superstar. Julie Christie won an Oscar in John Schlesinger's *Darling*, her fifth film.

As a schoolboy, Tom Courtenay, whose father chipped paint on the fishing boats at Hull, had failed the eleven-plus exam and therefore had no hope of going on to university. One of his teachers had recognized Courtenay's talent, however, and had had him write a special essay, which became the equivalent of an eleven-plus pass. Courtenay had then won a scholarship to London University, quickly found his way into acting, and given some unforgettable performances on stage and in film. Based on one such performance in *The Loneliness of the Long Distance Runner*, the editors at *Time* assigned me to interview him. We agreed to meet in the Coach and Horses pub next door to the Time-Life building. I'd never seen him on screen and didn't spot anyone who looked like an actor. Courtenay, who looked more like a messenger at the time, came up and asked rather shyly if I was the *Time* person. I later attended a morning screening (a most civilized British custom) of another of his films, Schlesinger's wonderful comedy about a compulsive fibber, *Billy Liar*. Courtenay was superb and so was the young woman who played a free-spirited young hippie on a visit to her provincial hometown—and who turned out to be Julie Christie. I was so impressed I rushed up to Nottingham, where Christie was a member of the local repertory company and living in a two-pounds-a-week boardinghouse, to interview her. After my pieces on both Tom and Julie ran, I liked to think I'd introduced them both to American audiences.

When I found O'Toole in his favorite pub in Hampstead, where he lived, he'd just returned from finishing *Lawrence*. "On Monday," he told me, "I'm going down to the country for a week of high colonics. Eight months riding a camel has ruined my insides." I next saw O'Toole as a robust and even gymnastic Hamlet in the long-awaited opening production of the National Theater. The demand was so great I was lucky to get even standing-room tickets.

The birth of the National reflected a new surge of vitality in the British theater, as did the creation of the brand-new plays of angry social realism. It had all begun in the mid-1950s with John Osborne's *Look Back in Anger,* which had a working-class antihero. Suddenly the actors who spoke with plummy BBC accents were out of fashion. The accents of the working class in London and in the provinces as well now gave the British stage new vigor. Michael Caine once told me that, in the old days, if an actor had a Cockney accent (as Caine did and does), the best he could hope for was a role as a petty criminal who tugs his forelock and says to the policeman, "I'll go quiet, guv." Now, in these postwar years, the British theater was undergoing an almost revolutionary change. Osborne and later social realists became known as the "Angry Young Men" or the "Angries" and their work as "kitchen sink drama." Angry Arnold Wesker would stage a trilogy of his plays about the discontent of left-wing intellectuals with frustrated socialist ideals. We saw another of his plays and his first big hit in the West End, the abrasively funny *Chips with Everything.*

I discovered you learned as much about theater by sitting through plays that didn't work as you did from being thrilled by those that did. It was a remarkable learning experience.

The London office received a pair of tickets not only to almost every new play but also to many of the glorious operas and ballets at Covent Garden, whose productions were special and sumptuous treats. One evening, we watched Rudolf Nureyev debut as a permanent member of the Royal Ballet dancing "Le Corsaire," a twelve-minute piece that featured his unequaled gravity-defying leaps. The ovation lasted almost three times as long the dance. On a rather dif-

ferent evening, we went to the premiere of the American Sam Wana-
maker's production of *La Forza del Destino* It was an unusual staging
with a steeply raked set, and much of the action took place down
front. At the end of the soprano's first aria, there was a long silence.
Then a single voice rang out from one of the balconies saying, "Dis-
gusting!" I was astonished. I turned to the Englishwoman sitting
next to me and asked, "Does this happen very often?" "Oh, yes," she
said. "We English like our fun." (But it wasn't common at all. The incident made the front page of several papers the next day.) The cat-
calling got worse as the performance wore on, and the soprano was
loudly booed at the final curtain. What had happened was that, in
the first place, Covent Garden Opera had let go a Welsh baritone
with a large following, and it was his claque who'd contributed most
of the negative noise. And, in the second place, having announced a
well-regarded soprano and increased the ticket prices accordingly,
when she had to bow out, the management had hastily imported an
Italian soprano with no following at all—but had not then reduced
the prices. When apprised of the facts, I felt a strong retroactive sad-
ness for the soprano. She never had a chance.

I suppose the most conspicuous culture shock when we arrived
from a land of multiple television channels running twenty-four
hours a day was to find that Britain had only one, the BBC, known fa-
miliarly as "Auntie." Fred Allen, a radio star in America, came back
from a visit to England and said that BBC Radio was unique. "They
start at 7:00 in the morning with a lecture on how to stuff a field
mouse and just go on from there." BBC Television shut down every
day just after eleven P.M. with the "Epilogue," a few words of hope
and encouragement from a preacher of one faith or another. But the
BBC's splendid series, most notably the original black-and-white
Forsyte Saga, soon made their way onto American television.

In time, England acquired its first commercial channel, which set
up an interesting tension, with the BBC now careful not to come

across as too stuffy and stolid. At the same time, the existence of the BBC inhibited the commercial channel from dipping too far down-market. One remarkable night early in the competition between the two channels, the commercial channel ran a Greek drama in the original Greek, while the BBC carried a professional wrestling match. But somehow there was always plenty to watch—including *That Was the Week That Was,* one of the best evenings of satire that ever was and one that caused millions of Britishers to stay at home on Saturday night when the show aired. The program's master of ceremonies was David Frost, a young man just down from Cambridge—and just launching his considerable career.

I made no claim to be an art critic, although art was part of my beat and it was an important time for the London art world. One of my early assignments was doing a profile on a young provincial artist whose visual signature was his bright blond hair. Even before he graduated from the Royal College of Art, David Hockney was known to be an artist to watch, as he has been this last half century, or nearly so. With his heavy North Country accent, Hockney gave a charming interview. He was confident but never arrogant and I found that his paintings, even before he saw Los Angeles, had a vitality and enthusiastic openness to the world that they have even now. Many years later, I would run into him at an art opening in Los Angeles. When I started to introduce myself, he said, "I know, you're the *Time* guy. Nice to see you again." Hockney has lived in Los Angeles for many years. The amusing, friendly look of his beaches and swimming pools and colorful umbrellas, widely popular as prints and posters, has become his trademark.

An American named R. B. Kitaj had spent years in England after growing up in Cleveland, Ohio, where he'd established a reputation as one of the most exciting artists of his time. His work had become extremely expensive; some of his gorgeous pastels were fetching $50,000. I bought a collage, which was all that would fit into our budget. After his beautiful young wife died, Kitaj, like Hockney before him, moved to Los Angeles, where his son is a screenwriter.

There seemed to be fine sculptors everywhere in London, including Barbara Hepworth, who later died tragically in a fire in her studio in Cornwall, and the grand old man of sculpture, Henry Moore. A photographer and I spent a day with Moore at his country place at Much Haddam, where he worked on his massive pieces outdoors once they had been cast, so he could watch how their patinas subtly evolved over time. Although Moore was one of the most highly regarded sculptors in the world, he was an unprepossessing a man, who seemed to live only for the making of his art.

The most conspicuous artist in town was Francis Bacon, whose works would appreciate enormously in value after his death. I made an appointment to interview him at his mews in Chelsea. When I arrived, I found he'd been up half the night scrawling page after page of notes in red ink on a yellow pad, trying to figure out what to say to me about his work. So far as I could tell, he never reached a conclusion, although part of his difficulty may have been the special meanings he attached to words. He said, for example, that he had about decided to start a series of portraits of his friends. To me, "portraits" meant portraits, but not to Bacon. His new portraits, like the one he did of his friend Clement Freud, closely resembled his earlier paintings of popes with faces melting like wax in the hot sun. On the other hand, I felt that artists should not be expected to describe their work in words; the work must speak for itself or keep silent. Bacon's paintings are some of the most emotionally disturbing of the period, as near as his generation has come to genius.

The world of literature was also thriving in postwar Britain. Erroneously diagnosed with a fatal brain tumor, the fine novelist Anthony Burgess came home from his colonial posting as an educator in Malaya. To create some sort of legacy for his wife, he began to write furiously and produced five novels in a year before he discovered he'd been misdiagnosed. He'd have many more productive years of writing, which would give rise to his most famous novel, *A Clockwork Orange*. For the four hundredth anniversary of Shakespeare's birth, Burgess had written an imaginative biography, in which he'd identified the dark lady of the sonnets. I wanted to interview him at his flat in Chelsea, but he insisted on coming to my office for our talk. He arrived puffing a cigar, carrying a satchel full of books, and wearing an ankle-length overcoat against the bitter cold. Burgess was one of the most intriguing talkers I've ever known. His conversation ranged widely, from Algonquin Indian legends to further speculation about Shakespeare (about whom little is actually known). We hit it off and later met at the Café Royale, sacred to the memory of Oscar Wilde, where we ate, drank, and talked for four hours.

The novelist Kingsley Amis cast a critical eye on British higher education, satirizing ambition in the provincial universities in his novels *Lucky Jim* and *That Certain Feeling*. Amis, who had himself taught in the provinces, always seemed to me an adjunct to the Angry Young Men, though his targets were those in a slightly higher stratum of society, a new class of postwar academics created by the newer "red-brick" colleges, rather than by Oxford and Cambridge. These days, Amis is probably also identified as the father of Martin Amis, an angry young novelist and critic of a later generation.

One noon at a luncheon of the American Correspondents Association, the honored guest was Prince Philip. When asked why the British universities had so few places in comparison with those in the United States, the prince answered that the aim of British higher education was to train students for the last job they would hold in their lives, whereas the aim of American higher education was to train students for the first job they would hold. I thought the prince's snobbish answer, though partly true, undervalued the democratization of American higher education.

The most commercially successful author when I arrived in London was Ian Fleming, whose James Bond novels had made 007 known worldwide, and who'd actually been in the British secret service for a time, although probably without a license to kill. Fleming was hot literary news and *Time* sent me to interview him a day or two before the premiere of the second James Bond film, *From Russia with Love*. At the reception after the premiere screening, I caught sight of Fleming across the foyer. Towering above everybody else, he looked like an ad for high-priced tuxedos. I went over to congratulate him. "You know Willie Maugham, of course," he said of his companion. It was, indeed, W. Somerset Maugham, who was then almost ninety, with a face like wrinkled parchment. At a loss for words, I said, "What did you think of the film, Mr. Maugham?" "Oh, splendid," Maugham said. "Splendid."

I escaped from the lively arts long enough to research a cover story on a race driver named Jim Clark, then the top-rated driver in the world. It was a reporter's nightmare. Clark hated to talk, especially to journalists. For the most part, I had to rely on what his fellow drivers said about him. Racers, I was told, rate the speed at which a curve is taken on a scale of one to ten, ten being the maximum speed at which it can be taken. "The rest of us hope to hit ten once in a while," one of Clark's pals said. "Jim *practices* at ten."

In a desperate attempt to get Clark to talk, I finally invited him and some of his pals to a dinner the night before a French race, at a country inn they liked outside Rouen. I had the only four-door sedan in the crowd so everybody piled into my car. "If you think I'm going to drive a car containing five Grand Prix drivers," I told Jim, "you are out of your mind." So he took the wheel and I sat scrunched in the middle. His racing partner, Peter Arundel, whispered in my ear, "Good thinking. Jim hates to ride with anybody else at the wheel."

We all had a grand dinner, but I don't think I got a single usable quote. The next day, Clark's girlfriend, a lovely young American, flew in from England for the race. Jim's greeting was, "This is Chuck, the one I warned you about" (the one not to talk to if you can possibly avoid it).

I think some race drivers simply can't tell you how they do it. They just do it. Clark had learned to drive steering a tractor along the furrows of the family farm in Berwickshire, Scotland, from the time he was so short he had to stand behind the steering wheel. He was a family legend. He could drive anywhere under any conditions when he was still too short to sit.

After the French race, Clark went on to the German Grand Prix at Nürburgring, which is close to the Rhine south of Dusseldorf. That day, his car conked out on the third lap. There was nothing more for me to do. I drove back north on the autobahn toward the airport; when traffic got too heavy, I crossed the Rhine and turned onto a secondary road that ran along the west bank. Some of the road signs were strangely familiar: Lammersdorf, Rollesbroich, and Euskirchen. Euskirchen was where I'd been hit in early March 1945. Now that I was in a peacetime mode, it had simply not occurred to me that I was near my own history. I debated swinging off the road and heading for Euskirchen, only a few kilometers inland. But in my rush to make the five o'clock plane to London out of Dusseldorf, I drove on and never saw Euskirchen. As it turned out, the London flight was just taking off when I reached the airport and there wasn't another that night. So I stayed over in Dusseldorf, that remarkable city with its shiny glass towers built after the wartime bombing, and not far from them the ancient streets and taverns that had somehow survived the war.

My cover story ran but I never heard how or whether Clark liked it. I only saw him once more, when he came to Riverside to race. I said hello and he greeted me warmly, relieved, I felt sure, that I was no longer asking questions. Some time later, I read that Clark, practicing for the German Grand Prix, again at Nürburgring, was driving at high speed all by himself on the back stretch when his rear axle apparently failed. His car left the track, hit a tree, and he was killed instantly.

Jim Clark's death was ironic because he'd made a point of being an extremely cautious driver, preferring to start in front, in the pole position, or to get there as quickly as he could and stay there. But Grand Prix racing is undeniably a dangerous sport. Many of the drivers I met while in pursuit of Jim Clark have since been killed while racing.

By an extraordinary piece of luck, I stumbled onto what became the most important cultural story of my London years and a phenomenon that captured the whole world: the Beatles. The cable room in the Time-Life bureau was a bustling place. That day, as I walked by, one of the cable operators and his mates were celebrating a birthday by singing some parody lyrics of a song I'd never heard. I asked Barbara Simon, our wonderfully efficient office manager, what the song was. "It's 'She loves you, Yeah, Yeah, Yeah,' " she said. "It's the Beatles."

"Who are the Beatles?" I asked.

Barbara told me briefly but steered me to the bureau's library, run by the encyclopedic Margaret Skea. It was so early that neither the Beatles records nor the Fab Four themselves were yet known in America, although evidently there was one disk jockey in the Northwest who had acquired their first recording and was beating the drum for them.

There were already bulging files of clippings about the Beatles in the library and I read them all. I followed in print their extraordinary rise from the cellars of Liverpool to their unprecedented popularity. I put together some of the salient facts about them and their screaming teenage followers, including the fact that seven thousand kids had stood in the rain overnight to buy tickets to a Beatles concert. I cabled a suggestion about the Beatles to the "Showbiz" section of

Time. Three days later came the cabled response: "Showbiz bypassing Champlin suggestion obscure Liverpool rock group." It was probably the last time in their history that anyone thought of the Beatles as obscure.

I suggested a piece on the group at least twice more before Showbiz finally assigned the story. It was just in the nick of time. The Beatles were scheduled to begin their historic American trip and the Beatles phenomenon would sweep America.

One afternoon, the producer of what was to be the Beatles first film, *A Hard Day's Night,* an American named Walter Shenson, invited me to join him on some locations in London where the director, Richard Lester, was shooting the Fab Four being pursued by several hundred screaming young women. The scenes were planned but not scripted and there were moments when the Beatles, enjoying every minute of it, did seem to be escaping only narrowly with their clothes intact. Everything the Beatles touched turned to gold and that included *A Hard Day's Night.*

The 1960s and 1970s were a fertile time for the British arts, which made their mark all over the world. But the most significant and enduring marks of British creativity were made by the Beatles, the perfect embodiment of postwar British optimism and the vision of a classless society in which you didn't have to be born to wealth or speak with a BBC accent to make your way to the top of your world. Pop music had replaced the movies as the preferred fantasy of escape from the dull, working-class world.

All of our lives suffered a violent shock on that November day in 1963 when John Fitzgerald Kennedy was assassinated in Dallas. With the time difference between Dallas and London, it was late afternoon when someone in the cable room who had a radio playing caught the first brief bulletin that JFK had been shot. There were no further details for what seemed like a long time. Four of us had planned to have a quick dinner at a Chinese restaurant in Soho, then go on to Columbia's offices for a screening of Stanley Kubrick's *Dr. Strangelove.* As we left the restaurant, the proprietor said, "Sorry, your President die." We still couldn't believe it, but when we arrived at the Columbia offices, a young publicist I knew was standing in front of the door sobbing. He didn't have to say a thing. Disbelief had become the need to accept the unthinkable. We knew no more than the people at home what the assassination meant, how it had come about, what it portended, and in far-off London there was little we could do except report the British and Continental reaction. The news of Kennedy's death was shattering wherever one heard it, but in London there was the anxiety and the frustration of being so far from home.

A few weeks later, we were invited to the British government's memorial tribute to JFK in St. Paul's Cathedral. Royalty was well represented and the service began with a platoon of trumpeters in their bright red uniforms playing a long, brilliant fanfare that sent chills up and down our spines in the enormous, echoing interior. The age and majesty of the cathedral, it seemed to me, and the ceremonies themselves escorted John Fitzgerald Kennedy to his place in history. The martyred president, a lifelong Anglophile, would have loved it.

That December, our sixth child, Nancy, was born in Kingston Hospital. The British protocol was for new mothers to stay in the hospital for ten days; the reasoning was that so many of the new mothers would have no home help. To get the women back on their feet, there were calisthenics in the wards every morning. Peg, who'd grown used to three- or four-day hospital stays back in the States, was impatient to go home and made such a fuss, however politely, that she was allowed to leave after four days. She was driven home in an ambulance to find the other children waiting at the door to greet their mother and new sister, Nancy.

In 1964, my mother and my brother, Joe, came for a visit, giving my mother a chance to hold her newest grandchild. Mother had by now been cancer-free for sixteen years. But, not long after returning to the States, she was diagnosed with lymphatic cancer, one she could not defeat. She died just short of her sixty-seventh birthday, in January 1965.

Not long before I left London in early 1965, Winston Churchill died, at the age of ninety-one. From a friend's office on Fleet Street, my son Chuck and I watched the long funeral cortege as it made its slow way from St. Paul's Cathedral down Fleet Street and on to the river. From there, the body of the greatest Englishman of the twentieth century was borne in its coffin by ceremonial barge down the Thames to the small village of Woodstock near Blenheim Palace, where Churchill was born and would now be buried. It was all moving and melancholy—the close to a historic chapter in Britain's modern history.

On a Friday afternoon in 1965, I got a phone call from an old Los Angeles friend named Gene Sherman, who was then the *Los Angeles Times* man in London. His editors had sent him a memo asking that he check me out as a possible entertainment editor and columnist for the paper, but not tell me anything. As a good friend, Gene had ignored their second request.

On Monday morning, Leonard Riblett, an assistant managing editor at the *Times*, called from Los Angeles and outlined the job pretty much as Gene had described it to me. In a sort of minuet, Riblett said he wasn't actually offering me the job, but he needed to know whether, if he did offer it, I would take it. Luckily, Peg and I had had the weekend to think about things. We loved England and were not anxious to leave. On the other hand, I'd been doing largely anonymous group journalism for *Time* and *Life* for seventeen years. The offer of my own signed column three times a week back in Southern California, which we also loved, was an offer we agreed I couldn't refuse.

Riblett called again Wednesday morning and, without preamble, said, "How much are you going to cost us?" I hadn't thought about money. I did some frantic calculations in my head. I had to make more money than I'd been making—that was only right. I wasn't sure the newspapers paid as much as magazines, but when I asked for what amounted to something like 25 percent more than my salary at the time, Riblett immediately agreed. Damn! I said to myself, you should have asked for more.

But everything turned out well. I received a warm note from Henry Luce thanking me for my service to the magazines and prophesying that I would enjoy working at the *Los Angeles Times* because he knew the Chandler family and they were good people.

In the glory days, when one of the editorial staff had a child, the staffer received a handsome sterling silver porringer from Black, Starr, engraved with something like "To [name of child] from Henry R. Luce and the rest of his (or her) father's friends at Time-Life, Inc." By the time I left *Life*, my wife and I had six porringers at various stages of denting. I wrote Luce to thank him for his letter and to say, lightly I hoped, that obviously Peggy and I would have no more children because a child without a porringer would be a second-class citizen.

In quick time, I had another letter from Luce, this one from Arizona, and it said in part, "If, as the Chinese say, fortune smiles and you and your wife are blessed with another child, I hope you will see that I am informed because it is high time that the tradition was amended." The tradition did not have to be amended for us, but the gesture has warmed me ever since.

Time-Life, Inc., had footed the bill—and it was a substantial one—to ship us lock, stock, and upholstered furniture from Los Angeles to London. The *Los Angeles Times* now had agreed to ship our goods and chattels and us back to Los Angeles again.

I'd fantasized about being a professional writer all my young days. I'm not sure I ever dreamed of being a signed columnist in complete charge of my own work and my destiny, but I was about to enter that enviable, magical state.

Afterword

All we have is memory, someone once said, and it's true. Tangible things disappear, structures are torn down to make way for other structures. A street we thought we knew is suddenly unfamiliar. The flow of life as we lived it sifts through our fingers like sand at the beach. We tell ourselves we'll never forget a scene, a meeting, a face, a voice, a kiss. But, all too soon, we have only fading memories of them.

Much of the life I've described in these memoirs is no more. Although, from the highway, the white farmhouse in Cleveland, New York, still looks like it did when I arrived in 1942, it is occupied by strangers. Mother and my stepfather lie side by side in the small, lovely cemetery above the lake just east of town, not far from the rustic cabin where Reverend MacNish once lived. He, too, is memory, where I still see the gray chain of cigarette ashes down the front of his cardigan.

As A. E. Housman says in one of his elegiac poems, the lightfoot lads and the rose-lipped maidens of youth are asleep except in memory.

Memoirs are attempts to preserve something of memory when the tangibles it remembers are no more. The restaurant where I washed dishes is long gone. Mrs. Labby's boardinghouse burned to the ground and was never rebuilt. The bandstand is still to be seen in

202

the park at Hammondsport, but the old players can no longer be heard. The Time-Life building where I began my career has another corporate name now, and the newer, shinier Time-Life building, which I've never visited, stands a few blocks away, on Sixth Avenue.

If memory is all, it is also precious, worth trying to preserve, even in small, suggestive clues.

I've tried to capture intimations of twenty years of a life and a time remembered, hazier now that macular degeneration has dimmed my sight and made my pen stumble. But if I invoke my own special past, the scenes from a particular life, I may evoke memories in others. Memory is shot through with universals. We are all moving on the same continuum, hoping to remember our lives even as they sift through our fingers, like sand beside the sea.